ASHA

Susie Heal has moved all over the country, buying and selling property along the way, and has learned from experience how to identify potential problems and avoid them. She has written two books on buying and selling property – *Buying Your Home* (HarperCollins, 1996) and *Selling Your Home* (HarperCollins, 1995) – and this new book takes into account the many changes that have happened in the property market since then.

Susie has also run a letting agency and worked in conveyancing for more than ten years. She now lives in Somerset.

Also available from Constable & Robinson

How To Buy Property at Auction
The essential guide to winning propery and buy-to-let bargains
Samantha Collett

The Complete Guide to Property Investment in France
How to find, buy and let second homes and houses
Gerry FitzGerald

Investing in Stocks and Shares
A step-by-step guide to making money on the stock market
Dr John White

How to Pay Less for More
The consumer's guide to negotiating the best deals –
whatever you're buying
Marc Lockley

Planting Plans for Your Kitchen Garden
How to create a vegetable, herb and fruit garden in easy stages
Holly Farrell

Why Can't My Garden Look Like That?
Proven, easy ways to make a beautiful garden of your own
John Shortland

HOW TO BUY YOUR HOME AND SAVE MONEY

Use insider knowledge and know-how to cut costs and avoid expensive mistakes

Susie Heal

RIGHT WAY

Constable & Robinson Ltd
55–56 Russell Square
London WC1B 4HP
www.constablerobinson.com

First published in the UK by Right Way,
an imprint of Constable & Robinson, 2014

Text copyright © Susie Heal 2014
Illustrations copyright © Colin Shelbourn, www.shelbourn.com, 2014

NOTE: The material contained in this book is set out in good faith for general
guidance and no liability can be accepted for loss or expense incurred as a result
of relying in particular circumstances on statements made in the book. Laws and
regulations are complex and liable to change, and readers should check the
current position with relevant authorities before making personal arrangements.

A copy of the British Library Cataloguing in Publication Data
is available from the British Library

ISBN: 978-0-71602-380-7 (paperback)
ISBN: 978-0-71602-381-4 (ebook)

1 3 5 7 9 10 8 6 4 2

CONTENTS

FOREWORD

Ever wondered why some people sail through life's challenges easily, whilst others have stress and problems right from the start? The answer is simple. The first group know what they're doing; the others stumble through on a wing and a prayer.

When it comes to buying a home, you really do need to know what you're doing. At a time when mortgages are difficult to find, house prices are unpredictable and the property market is in turmoil, the need to make a good investment is paramount. This book can help, with simple, easy-to-understand information, in one place, for the whole process. No more trying to piece together bits of data from several sources. This is a concise guide to making the right choices and saving money along the way; from finding the right property through to planning a stress-free moving day.

The book covers all areas of buying a home, whether you are doing it for the first time, or want to improve on your last experience. It is also full of practical advice to ensure a wise investment for minimum cost. That's the unique part of this book, and I don't think there is another quite like it.

You can learn about:

- Finding the right property for you, without spending more than you need.
- Funding, and how to avoid some of the fees and charges involved.
- The need for a survey, and how it can save you money in the long run.
- Conveyancing, and how to get the most out of your solicitor.
- The pros and cons of buying at auction, and how to go about it.
- Leases, new homes and buying with a partner.
- How to have a hassle-free move.

Chapter 1

FINDING THE RIGHT PROPERTY

NEEDS AND WANTS

Caveat Emptor – 'let the buyer beware'. This is an appropriate way to start this book because it's worth noting that, unlike retail purchases, you do not have a host of consumer protection rights to protect your interests when you buy a property. You have no opportunity to exchange it or get a refund if you decide you don't like it, and if it's not 'fit for purpose' you have no rights to claim against the seller. There is no 'cooling-off period' during which you can change your mind, and with the exception of newly constructed buildings, there are no guarantees or warranties.

All of this means that it's vital to buy wisely, and in order to do so you need to decide *before* you start looking for the perfect home exactly what it is you want and need. This will go some way towards saving you from being swept away by emotions and buying something appealing, but ultimately impractical.

If you are buying jointly, with a friend or partner, or if you are moving as a family, you will all need to agree on what you need from your new home. Prioritize those aspects of your home that are vital, and those that are preferable – your needs and wants. For example:

Needs	Wants
Price under £180,000	Large garden
3 bedrooms or more	Kitchen/diner
On bus route	Conservatory
Off-street parking	Garage

Once you have found several properties that meet your needs, all you have to do is decide which one has that little something extra from your wants list.

You may be tempted to compromise on one of your needs if a particular property bowls you over, but always keep in mind the necessities. Aesthetic qualities are all very well, but practical requirements are ultimately more important for long-term happiness. No matter how wonderful the kitchen is, or how beautifully tended the garden, these relatively minor aspects will soon lose their appeal if the property is in the wrong area, is too small or is more expensive than you can comfortably afford.

MONEY-SAVING TIP
Consider the lifespan of anything you feel tempted to pay extra for, like extravagant decoration. High mortgage repayments will continue to be a financial burden long after the paint has faded.

CHOOSING WISELY

Buying a home is, of course, the most important and most expensive purchase we ever make. And yet many people enter into the process completely unprepared and ill informed, with the result that their purchase is disappointing and ultimately doesn't suit them.

More questions have been asked and more books have been written about selling a home than about buying one. But, if you buy a property wisely in the first place, you should have no trouble selling it when the time comes.

What's surprising is that it's not only first-time buyers who fall into purchasing mishaps: it's often the more experienced buyers who, complacent as they have 'done it all before', make fundamental mistakes. Let's take a look at a few.

The gullible buyer

A gullible buyer naively believes everything he or she reads or is told about a property, regardless of the obvious fact that such information is supplied by those who are hoping to sell it (the current owner and selling agents) and who are understandably somewhat biased.

Thankfully, and not before time, the Property Misdescriptions Act, or more recently Consumer Protection from Unfair Trading Regulations (CPRs), have gone some way towards stamping out the kind of elaborate and largely inaccurate property descriptions that used to be commonplace. Because of these regulations, estate agents, developers, builders and solicitors are all responsible for the accuracy of any information they give to potential buyers.

Nevertheless, buyers still need to interpret correctly the information they receive, be satisfied that they know exactly what they are buying, and not deceive themselves by turning a blind eye to some disagreeable aspect of a property.

The trusting buyer

This buyer makes poor decisions because he believes that there are rules to protect him from unscrupulous sellers or defective properties. Not true. A trusting buyer imagines that consumer laws extend to property purchases, so he makes little effort to protect himself.

The laws that protect retail consumers do not cover property purchases, so there is no one to turn to if a property turns out to be 'faulty'. If you buy a bucket that does not hold water, it is clearly unfit for the purpose for which it was sold, and you have grounds for asking for a refund or replacement. But a property with a leaking roof is not covered by the same statutory rights. In theory, a buyer can sue a negligent surveyor who fails to point out serious defects in the property, but the procedure is lengthy, complicated, expensive and carries no guarantee of success.

So, as far as a property purchase is concerned, responsibility for ensuring the 'product' is suitable rests ultimately with the buyer alone.

The lazy buyer

The lazy buyer cannot be bothered to put much effort into finding the right property and buys the first thing that comes along. He's likely to discover too late that the property does not fit his requirements, and he stands very little chance of securing a good investment.

The bankrupt buyer

Being unrealistic when calculating what you can afford, or going into unmanageable debt because of temptation, is a recipe for financial disaster. It stands to reason that the more expensive a property is, the more desirable it is likely to be. Rather than accepting his financial limitations, the bankrupt buyer persuades himself that he can afford additional debt, or is prepared to be without a car, a holiday, or other luxuries, in order to afford the repayments. The end result is at best unhappiness, and at worst repossession.

The gambler
The gambler assumes the value of the property he buys will rise, and calculates his finances accordingly. This assumption carries a huge risk. The gambler should remember that property values can fall, which could leave him owing more on a mortgage than the property is worth (see Negative equity, page 60).

WILL IT SELL?

Without a doubt, the biggest consideration to take on board when choosing a property is whether or not you could sell it reasonably easily if you needed to, preferably without losing money in the process. Amazingly this is something that doesn't cross the minds of many people.

Think about it: if you find a property you like, but you discover the current owners have been struggling to sell it for some considerable time, you stand a good chance of finding yourself in the same position in the future, when you come to sell it. It may be that you would be able to wait for a buyer to come along, but if you had to sell quickly, would you be able to?

The exception to this would be a property that has not sold because it is in poor condition. Provided the price reflects the present condition, and this is the *only* reason it has been slow to sell, then you should find it easier to sell after making the necessary improvements.

Don't expect the agent or seller to be totally honest and volunteer the information about how long a property has been on the market, and bear in mind it could have been for sale with other agents before switching to the current one. Exterior photographs on the details can offer valuable clues to the season when the property was first marketed. If it has been on the market for many months, ask yourself why.

It's not difficult to see what makes a property easy to sell – visual appeal, a good location and a fair price are the top three points. So turning these things on their head gives you a good idea of what makes a property *difficult* to sell.

Location is all important, and in particular the immediate surroundings. A property next to anything unsightly, like a petrol station or car park, or near noise or disturbance, like a pub or chip shop, comes high on the list of undesirable locations. Busy roads, neighbourhoods which are out of favour and nearby property in disrepair are all generally worth avoiding. You may be content to put up with something unpopular, but will anyone else when you come to sell?

Bear in mind also that if you find your lender is reluctant to fund a particular purchase, any future buyers could experience the same problems.

WHAT TYPE OF BUILDING?

When deciding on what type of property is best for you, you will need to consider the pros and cons of different building styles.

If your priorities are peace and quiet, and you are willing to pay the price, a detached house might be right for you to avoid noise from attached properties. Semi-detached and terraced homes are generally cheaper, but have the disadvantage of close neighbours and the accompanying noise this can bring. You may consider, however, that close neighbours are both a security and a social advantage.

Flats rarely have private outside space, but this could be a plus if you do not have the time or energy to look after a garden. Flats are generally leasehold, and the lease will almost certainly contain restrictions on the use of the property, so make sure you read this carefully as, for example, you may not be allowed to keep pets.

External repair and maintenance of the building is not usually the direct responsibility of the leaseholder, but maintenance costs and service charges can be high.

Older properties are often more popular than their modern counterparts. They are generally built on a larger plot, allowing more space between neighbours and offering bigger gardens. However, they were not constructed with en-suite bathrooms and built-in storage as standard, and may not have the high grade insulation common to modern buildings.

HOW MUCH TO SPEND?

Home buyers often borrow as much as they possibly can, either because they anticipate their investment increasing (the bigger the investment the bigger the potential increase, in theory at least) or because property is so expensive that borrowing a large proportion of the purchase price is the only way many people can fund a purchase at all.

But the question buyers should always ask themselves is 'How much can I afford to borrow?' not 'What is the maximum I can borrow?'

MONEY-SAVING TIP
You do not have to buy the most expensive home you can afford.
If a cheaper property meets your needs, why pay more?

Deciding how much to pay for a property is not only a matter of how much you can borrow. It also depends on:

- **Your monthly outgoings** How much can you comfortably afford to spend on mortgage repayments when added to your other living expenses?

- **How much debt you feel confident to carry** If you are concerned about job security, for example, consider the financial impact of job loss or changing employers before deciding how much to borrow, and perhaps take out suitable insurance.
- **Your future needs** If you intend to extend your family, for instance, it might be more cost effective to buy a larger property in the first place, rather than incurring a second set of sale and purchase costs when you need to move to get more space.
- **The costs involved in a purchase** Conveyancing costs, mortgage fees, survey fees, Stamp Duty, removal charges and more – all on top of the purchase price itself – may eat away at the funds you intend to use towards the cost of the purchase. Factor in everything you will need to spend and decide whether you will need to borrow more than originally planned, or else choose a slightly cheaper property.

> **MONEY-SAVING TIP**
> There are several websites offering free budget planning. Simply enter your income and outgoings to get a realistic view on what you can afford. It only takes a few minutes, but if you are intending to take out a loan or mortgage, it's a really useful tool to avoid over stretching your finances.

Be realistic about how much you can afford to borrow. In 2011, an estimated 800,000 British homes were in negative equity, meaning that the property was actually worth less than the loan secured on it.

Decide how much you want (and can afford) to spend and then speak to your lender. Arrange provisional funding and then look for property up to that amount. That way you start your property search knowing your upper limit, instead of wasting time looking at (and being tempted by) properties you cannot really afford.

MONEY-SAVING TIP

It's not easy, but if you can buy below £125,000 you will avoid Stamp Duty.

SEARCHING THE MARKET

Your first step in the hunt for the ideal property will probably be to visit local estate agents and sign up to the various online sites to find out what properties are currently for sale. Decide on your search area and drive round the local streets at different times of day to help get an idea of which areas you like best, and whether there are any you want to avoid.

USING ESTATE AGENTS

Do not rely on estate agents to understand what you want, need or can afford, or to give reliable information about areas, an individual property or the position – financial or otherwise – of the sellers. Remember, they are working on behalf of the vendor to sell the property. Neither should estate agents be relied upon for financial advice, although many of them do have mortgage advisers as part of their team.

Estate agents and property sites show what property is available at the time. Keep to the forefront of your mind that estate agents are there purely to sell property – it is of no concern to them who buys it. A satisfied buyer is not nearly as important as a satisfied seller, since it is the seller who pays the agent's fee.

Registering with agents

Registering with an agent is a simple process. Telephone, call in or email them with your contact details and information about the type of property you are looking for. They will then send you details of any relevant properties they have on their books, and arrange for you to view any that interest you.

You may receive details of the same property from several different agents, or see it on several websites, and if this happens it doesn't matter which agent you approach to arrange a viewing.

Agents often specialize in a particular type of property, with some selling mostly lower-priced property, while others deal exclusively with rural property or the higher end of the market.

To ensure that you don't miss a suitable property, register with as many agents and online sites as possible. Try to be flexible when setting the criteria of what you are looking for. If you say you are looking for an older-style semi, you may not get details of terraced, detached or modern properties at all. If you say you only need three bedrooms, you may not get details of those with four. It is better to give a broad brief rather than miss out on something which in retrospect you would have considered, had you known about it.

> **MONEY-SAVING TIP**
>
> Agents will routinely ask what your maximum purchase price is, and mostly send details of property at or above this figure. This means you could miss out on a perfectly suitable property that is cheaper than your maximum figure. Ask for details of property within a wide price range. This way you may find the home you want for less than you thought.

Once you begin to get a feel for what is available, you can narrow your requirements, firmly establishing exactly what you hope to find in a property, and telling the agents so that they can help you find it.

Keep in contact with the agents you register with. They tire of sending out property details to applicants they never hear from, and you run the risk of being forgotten if you do not show that you are genuinely keen to buy. Make sure you are easily contactable too, so that you can be the first to hear of new property on the market. Some of the best property is sold before the details are even printed.

After each viewing, report back to the agents, letting them know what you did or did not like about the property, and reaffirming what you are looking for.

USING THE INTERNET

There are many Internet sites worth visiting. These are basically a promotional tool used by estate agents, but they are also a great way of keeping up to date with what property is available in the area, and the price trends. You can register with these sites (or search them) very easily and you can often sign up for alerts when new property meeting your requirements get added. They also give details of estate agents in your area, although not all the agents may be listed.

In addition, there are various sites offering 'private house sales'. These are essentially estate agents without shop fronts. Sellers are attracted by the low selling costs, and their property is listed on the site in much the same way as with estate agents, with photographs, details of room sizes and all the other information you would expect. There will be a telephone number to call if you want to arrange any viewings.

The disadvantage of these sites is that the person on the end of the phone may not have visited the property. They may not even have local knowledge, so if you want to ask about something that is not shown in the details, like proximity of schools or ease of public transport, they may not know the answer.

MONEY-SAVING TIP

Become an expert on local property prices. Online sites give information on 'for sale' property prices in the area, but perhaps of more use are the sites showing sold prices, such as Nethouseprices.com and OurProperty.co.uk

INDEPENDENT SELLERS

Some sellers prefer to advertise their property themselves, either on the Internet through sites like HouseWeb or by other means, usually spurred on by the idea of avoiding estate-agency fees. Self-marketing can be as low tech as dropping leaflets through doors, posting an advert on the local post office or shop notice board, or taking out an advert in the local press.

If you find a property of interest advertised like this, you will need to arrange to view it directly with the sellers, and then negotiate a price with them if you are interested in buying it. Once you have agreed a price, swap details of your respective solicitors, and then the process will be much the same as if an agent was involved.

Ordinarily the estate agent acts as go-between, eliminating the need for direct contact between buyer and seller. In this situation, though, you will either have to address minor queries through your solicitors, or contact the sellers direct.

You must advise your solicitor of any arrangements you make with the sellers, whether it concerns fixtures and fittings, moving dates or anything else, so that he can confirm them with the seller's solicitor. Never rely on verbal agreements, even made with a handshake, as they are impossible to prove should the seller go back on his word.

The conveyancing process is the same as buying through an agent, although you must, in the absence of written details prepared by an estate agent, provide your solicitor with as much information about the property as possible. It is a good idea to take some photographs of the property, and give copies to your solicitor. He will then be alerted to, for example, a shared driveway, and can make enquiries about it on your behalf.

VIEWINGS

This is your chance to try before you buy. Most people decide very quickly whether a property is right for them or not, but you don't need to be rushed. Take your time during viewings and make the most of them. But before you can even think about arranging any viewings, first you need to decide which properties are worth turning out for.

Unless you are looking for something very specific, you will find dozens of potentially ideal properties for sale. At first, most of them will seem, on paper at least, to be likely candidates for viewing. So how do you start to find your ideal needle in this property haystack?

It helps, when faced with so many properties, to sort them into categories – the best, the not so good and the reserves (the good, the bad and the ugly, if you like). Don't be overwhelmed. The number will be slimmed down as you find out more about each property, so in the early stages it's best not to dismiss too many out of hand.

Don't throw away any of the written details until you have made a final choice. You may need to reconsider 'reserve' properties if your initial selection proves disappointing.

Before arranging any viewing appointments, it is worth taking a look at suitable properties from the outside. Even a cursory glance will be more enlightening than the selling agent's photograph, and you get the chance to find out exactly where each property is situated and what is around it. Make a note of anything that needs immediate clarification, and ask the agent for further information before arranging a viewing.

To arrange a viewing, simply ask the relevant agent to make an appointment with the sellers. If the agent is marketing several properties that interest you, you could ask for a schedule of viewings to be arranged, so that you can go from one property to the next. Each viewing will probably take around half an hour. If you do not know the area (and even if you do) the agent may be willing to transport you between viewings, particularly if they are going to show you round the properties themselves.

Most sellers choose to conduct viewings themselves, rather than let the agents handle it. Some sellers are good at this, giving just the right amount of information about the property and area. Others either bombard you with over-enthusiastic chit chat or are completely uncommunicative. Don't be put off buying a property by the personality of the sellers: remember, they are not included in the price.

MAKE THE MOST OF YOUR VIEWING

When arriving for a viewing, allow enough time to drive or walk around the immediate vicinity. This gives you an opportunity to observe the comings and goings of the neighbourhood, and you could uncover something detrimental, like a lot of passing traffic or even offensive smells, which might not be noticeable from inside the house.

Don't limit your observations to an internal inspection. Take a good look at the outside of the property as well, and take stock of the state of repair. You do not need to be a surveyor to notice neglect. Peeling paint, crumbling garden walls, loose guttering or damaged roof tiles tell more about the general condition of a property than internal decoration, which may well have been tidied up with a lick of paint, ready for the sale.

Once inside, you may get an instant impression, which is either good or bad. If you feel immediately negative about a property it is probably worth trusting your instincts, although try not to dismiss a basically sound and suitable property just because the decoration is not to your taste. If redecorating is necessary, the cost will need to be built into your budget, but ultimately the suitability of the accommodation and location are more important than the colour of the wallpaper.

If you feel immediately positive about a property, again trust your instincts, but try not to be bowled over by aesthetics. Keep your needs firmly in mind, and satisfy yourself that your basic criteria are being met.

Aim to find out as much as possible during a viewing. Firstly, look around carefully, ignoring the current owner's furniture and effects, because they are immaterial. Look at the proportions of each room. Would your furniture fit? Look at the general condition. Is it sound? What is the state of the ceilings? Are they water stained or cracked? Are the window frames in good repair? What about the heating? Are there enough radiators, and is the boiler modern?

As you move from room to room, you will be able to establish exactly what fixtures and fittings are included in the purchase price. If you decide to buy the property, the seller will be required to submit a list of these, which will be legally binding.

Don't be afraid to ask questions about anything that is not immediately visible, such as loft space or the garage. You may also want information about running costs. If this is important to you, be sure to get copy bills. Don't rely on the seller's verbal assurance that the bills are 'quite low'.

If you forget to ask something during a viewing, contact the agent afterwards and ask him to find out the answer for you. If you're still interested in the property, a second viewing (which is highly recommended) will give you the opportunity to ask the seller more specific questions.

If the seller mentions any treatments performed on the property, for example against damp or woodworm infestation, be sure to ask your solicitor to obtain guarantees if you decide to go ahead with the purchase.

You may have quite a few properties to view, some of them very similar, and this can become confusing. To keep each property fresh in your mind, jot down notes during each viewing. The agency details will already give you basic information but they cannot cover everything, so scribbling a few additional notes on the agency details will be enormously helpful when you come to review the properties you have seen. Making notes not only serves as a reminder long after the event, but also helps to focus on what you saw.

Try to find out how motivated the sellers are. Have they found a new home to move to? How quickly do they plan to move? If they are buying a new-build property, when will it be ready? The selling agents usually know their client's plans (or think they do), but they might not volunteer something that could put you off the purchase, so information direct from the sellers is often more revealing.

Lastly, many people feel obliged to put on a poker face during viewings, fearing a show of enthusiasm could push the price up. In reality, a seller is more likely to negotiate with someone who seems genuinely keen to buy than he is with someone whose 'take it or leave it' attitude inspires little confidence that negotiations will result in a sale.

SECOND VIEWINGS

When you find a property that interests you, always go back for a second look before putting in an offer to buy. Curiously, most people like a property less the second time they view it, so don't be surprised if your follow-up visit doesn't impress as much as the first. It simply means you are looking with your eyes rather than your emotions.

If the seller was uncommunicative during the initial viewing, visiting a second time might be more productive, because the atmosphere is often less formal. The seller feels confident that you are seriously considering buying, and you will feel more comfortable in surroundings that are now familiar. As a bonus, you may be encouraged to view at your own pace, unsupervised, which gives you the opportunity to look around without distraction.

Arrange your second viewing at a different time of day and on a different day of the week from the first. The road that was so quiet on a Sunday could be a rat run for commuters on a weekday morning or afternoon.

A second viewing is usually less emotionally driven. You will already know what the property has to offer, and you can now take a really good look at the building itself with a clear head.

RELOCATING

Finding the right property can be difficult at the best of times, but moving to a new area brings added complications. You will not be familiar with local property values, available transport, nearby schools, or all the other amenities. Perhaps most importantly, your knowledge of the areas that are desirable, and those which are less so, will be limited.

There is also a risk that you could be rushed into making a decision simply because journeying to view properties is difficult and time consuming. If you are aware of these potential pitfalls, you can go a long way to avoid them with good planning and some homework, before getting to the stage of trundling up the motorway to view individual properties.

START LOOKING FROM HOME

First things first. Search online for agents who operate in the area, or if you don't have Internet access get hold of a local newspaper with a property section, then you can register as a potential buyer without leaving home. Rather than telephoning the agents, it's simpler to write or email, explaining that you are moving to the area and listing your basic requirements, including price range, type of property, number of bedrooms and any other key essentials. This saves repeating yourself over the telephone, and is more reliable than leaving it to whoever answers the phone to make accurate notes of what you are looking for.

When you do visit the area, call into the estate-agency offices. You can then speak to the agents direct, and collect details of any properties that seem suitable while you are there. You'll often find you get better service when an agent has met you in person and can put a face to one of the many names that come across his or her desk each day. You can also get some valuable local knowledge and perhaps even a street map.

You should already have a good idea of the type of property you are looking for, and you can get a feel for current prices in the area by studying the online sites. At this stage it pays to be flexible in your requirements, at least until you know what is available.

Property prices vary enormously in different parts of the country, so you may have either a pleasant surprise or a nasty shock.

> **MONEY-SAVING TIP**
> Prices will differ between neighbouring villages and towns, so if your chosen location seems expensive, look at those nearby, as you may have inadvertently selected the most expensive in the area.

Before you start to plough through the agency details, it's helpful to have a map of the town or area so that you can see where each property is situated. You can then begin to familiarize yourself with the peculiarities of each part of the town or locality. You may notice, for example, a large proportion of properties for sale in the same streets or estates, indicating a dense and transient population. The most sought-after areas will be those where property rarely comes onto the market, and of course the prices will be higher.

A map will also be invaluable when you come to arrange a schedule of viewings, helping you to plan a route to visit one property after another without criss-crossing the area needlessly, or allowing too little time to get from one viewing to the next.

If newly built homes are of interest to you, there are many new home sites up and down the country, so you may have several sites to choose from. At the time of writing, the construction industry is going through a particularly hard time, but from the buyer's point of view this means that new homes are often offered with attractive incentive packages.

Not all new homes are sold through estate agents, and some building companies prefer to deal with sales directly. You can get details of new sites by searching online. They are often on the edge of towns or villages. (See Chapter 6, Buying a Newly Built Home.)

GET TO KNOW THE AREA

When you visit the area you are moving to, try to stay for a few days to familiarize yourself with the locality. This is especially useful if you are not tied to moving to a particular town but have the choice of several. The more choices you have, the longer it will take to explore, but the higher your chances will be of finding what you want at the price you can afford.

- Give yourself enough time to get a feel for the area. Talk to the locals – are they friendly and enthusiastic about their town? In rural areas, the local pub is a good place to get information about the surrounding villages and the amenities each has to recommend it.
- Take time to walk around the town or just sit on a bench and watch the comings and goings. You can learn a lot from simply observing your surroundings. Does the town centre seem to be thriving, with plenty of activity? Look at the people and you will usually get some idea of the predominant age group and social condition of the population.
- Find out if your interests are catered for: whether there are restaurants, cinemas, places to walk the dog, or whatever you need from an area. If you have children, what schools are available, and where are the best ones situated?
- Visit the local library or tourist information office if there is one, and pick up any available literature on the area and local things to do.
- If you are moving with your job, ask your new colleagues which areas they recommend. You will gradually start to build up a picture of the different parts of town or different villages. Personal opinions vary, but if you speak to enough people you will begin to get an idea of how the area is arranged and what it has to offer.

- If you will be travelling to work, test the route, preferably during rush hour, to see how long it takes. This can be deceptive and sometimes a trip across town can take more time than a journey from a village, which may involve more mileage but less traffic congestion.

A lack of local knowledge makes second viewings even more important than usual, not only to double check that a specific property is right for you, but also to look at the street and general area at different times of the day and on different days of the week. You do not want to buy a home in what appears at first sight to be a quiet cul-de-sac, only to discover that it becomes a playground for noisy children at the weekend.

IN SUMMARY

- Only buy a property you could sell reasonably easily if you needed to.
- Don't lose sight of your priorities.
- Don't borrow what you cannot comfortably afford to repay.
- Don't buy what you cannot afford (in time as well as money) to repair and maintain.
- Don't be tempted by aesthetics that will fade.
- Always visit a property you like at least twice, preferably at different times of the day and on different days of the week.
- Don't be rushed into a decision by estate agents or sellers.
- Don't be persuaded that a property could fit your requirements if you do this or that. If you need a garage, make sure you get one; don't accept the seller's assurance that the area on the side of a property could be put to this use unless there is planning permission and the price allows for construction.
- Satisfy yourself that you have seen all suitable properties before you make a decision. Don't buy the first one that meets your minimum criteria.
- Don't view a property as an island. Remember that the surrounding area and adjacent properties affect the overall environment, especially where flats are concerned because the common parts, such as hallways and gardens, directly impact on all the flats in the block.
- Compare prices carefully and be thorough when looking at exactly what you get for your money in comparison with other similar properties.
- View properties in daylight.

Chapter 2
MAKING AN OFFER, AND CHAINS

NEGOTIATING AN OFFER

Once you have found your ideal home, it's time to negotiate the price. It's essential that you know the *real* value of the property before you pick up the phone and place your offer on the table. In other words, you should know, from your own observations and research, what the property is worth, regardless of what the asking price is.

In this day and age, it's not difficult. Check out sites like Zoopla, Rightmove and the Land Registry for sold prices in the area, and you'll soon be well versed in price trends.

MONEY-SAVING TIP

Don't be shy of offering less than the asking price. The sellers may refuse your first offer, but then again they may not. In any event, you'll find out what their bottom line is.

If the property has only just come onto the market, the sellers are unlikely to accept the first offer they receive (if it is lower than the asking price) because they could then miss out on a higher offer in future weeks or months. Find out from the agents how long the property has been for sale – if it's more than normal for the area, the sellers may be open to offers.

Of course current market values will give you an idea of how much to offer, but you must also decide what the property is worth to you personally. You may feel so passionately about a particular property that you are prepared to pay an inflated price for it. Bear in mind though, that you will lose money when you try to sell it if you cannot find an equally enthusiastic buyer. On the flip side, there is no point paying extra for an expensive feature that you do not particularly want. If you like a property but not the price, offer only what it is worth to you.

Often during viewings, sellers hint at the amount they are prepared to sell for, and they may indicate whether they are keen to sell quickly, which could work in your favour. Most sellers just want to achieve a good price with the least amount of hassle. If your offer is reasonable, and you are in a position to proceed without delay, it will probably be accepted.

MONEY-SAVING TIP

When you make an offer, leave some room for negotiation. If your offer is the maximum you can afford, you cannot increase it even if you would like to.

Offers are usually made through the selling agent, verbally in the first instance, or to the seller direct. Speak to the agents and find out as much as possible about the sellers and the property. Try to find out how long the property has been on the market and whether the sellers have had many second viewings. The agents probably won't tell you what they feel the sellers are willing to accept, although they may indicate that they are open to offers in the hope of encouraging you to make one.

Try to find out why the property is being sold, whether the sale is urgent and if the sellers have found another property to buy, which they could lose if their own sale does not proceed. This will give you an idea of how receptive they may be to a reduced offer.

Also, check out the Hometrack housing-market site to see the percentage of asking prices achieved in your area. At the moment, on average, property sells for around 94 per cent of the asking price, so realistically you can take at least 6 per cent off the asking price when you make your first offer.

AGREEING THE FINAL PRICE

Ultimately, you will need to negotiate if you want to get a good deal. Remember it's the agent's job to get the property sold as quickly as possible and for the best price, so prepare your argument for putting in a reduced offer before you make it.

Let's look at a good negotiating scenario. You find a house that's being offered for sale at £225,000 but you want to pay a maximum £205,000.

You   'We really like this property, but it's £25,000 more than similar ones we've seen. We would like to offer £200,000. Our mortgage is arranged and our own property is sold, so we can move quickly.'

Agent   'I'm afraid your offer is refused – will you increase your offer?'

You   'We feel the property is over-priced; however, we would
be prepared to offer £3,000 more, but this is stretching
our budget.'

Agent   'Your offer is still refused – will you increase your offer
any more?'

You   'The maximum we can raise is £205,000. We are
prepared to offer that if the sellers include X, Y and Z in
the sale [curtains, kitchen items perhaps]. Remember,
our own property is sold, so we can move quickly.'

Agent   'Your offer is accepted.'

Result   You have the property for the price you wanted, plus
some extras, and of course it's possible your original offer
might have been accepted.

MONEY-SAVING TIP

Give the agents a reduced budget to work with. During negotiations,
they will indicate this to the sellers, who may be more likely to
accept your offer if they know you can't go any higher.

SEALING THE DEAL

An offer is not binding until contracts are exchanged (see Chapter
8, Conveyancing). Therefore, you can make an offer and then
retract or reduce it if, for example, a survey down-values the
property, or if it raises expensive repair issues. In such cases you
might decide to withdraw from the purchase altogether, or reduce
your offer to take account of the altered circumstances.

If you reduce your offer because of necessary repairs, put together
reasonable evidence in the form of estimates or quotes to
substantiate the reduction. The sellers know the same problems will
surface with any future buyer, so they will usually be happy to allow

access for contractors to assess the job and will be keen to work something out.

Such is the risk of a buyer withdrawing (a property can be 'sold' several times before finally completing) that sellers often leave their property on the market until contracts are exchanged. This means the property continues to be available and any further interested buyers are held in reserve in case the original sale falls through. If a higher offer is received, then the seller may well withdraw from the original sale and accept the higher offer, a process known as 'gazumping'.

To protect against being gazumped, you need to show that you are a serious buyer and in a position to proceed quickly. So, arrange your mortgage funding in principle before making an offer, and do everything in your power to keep the administration side of things moving smoothly. You could also make your offer conditional on the property being withdrawn from the market. The sellers may or may not agree to this, but it's certainly worth asking.

Chapter 8 gives some advice on how to work with your solicitor to help him complete the legal work quickly, and you may need to pester your lender and surveyor to avoid delays.

MONEY-SAVING TIP

Don't let the agents know you are desperate to find a property quickly. If the sellers hear of this they will have the upper hand in price negotiations.

Finally, if your chosen property is in need of modernization, or if it will only meet your requirements after some sort of conversion, you need to calculate the cost of this before deciding how much to offer.

The cost of improvements can be much more than anticipated. For example, if you are intending to install a new kitchen, there will be expenses for fitting, plumbing, electrical work, carpentry and maybe decoration, all on top of the cost of the kitchen units. You will also need to check whether planning permission is required for any major alterations and, if so, be reasonably assured by the relevant authorities that it will be granted on application.

You can apply for planning permission on a property that you do not own, or contact the council's local planning department, explain what you are hoping to do and get their opinion on whether permission would be needed, and if it's likely to be granted. This is only a guideline, of course, and no guarantee that your actual application would be approved.

If you are planning an extension or loft conversion, for example, look at other houses nearby. If extensions or loft conversions are commonplace, then you can be reasonably assured that permission will be granted.

CHAINS

Sale and purchase transactions often fail through no fault of the seller or buyer, but simply because the 'chain' breaks down. A 'chain' is a term used to describe a series of simultaneous transactions, likening them to links in a chain.

A PROPERTY CHAIN

The end of the chain

Mr and Mrs C are buying a new-build home

▼

Mrs B is buying from Mr and Mrs C

▼

Mr A is buying from Mrs B. He has no property to sell.

The start of the chain

The example in the box opposite is of a very small chain with only three links, so it would stand a good chance of success. But if any 'link' pulls out of the chain, the whole series of transactions breaks down. For example, if Mrs B withdraws because she cannot raise sufficient funds, then Mr A has nothing to buy, and Mr and Mrs C lose their buyer.

Because so many failed purchases are the result of broken chains, you might like to find out from the agents about the length and complexity of the chain you would become involved in before making an offer on a particular property. If it is very long or shows signs of difficulty, such as a buyer who has already pulled out of previous purchases, or a vendor who still has to find a property to move to, this could reflect on your decision to buy. You could spend a lot of money on arranging a mortgage, surveys and solicitor costs, only to find that you can no longer proceed because of something out of your control. The selling agents are usually able to advise how many transactions are involved in a chain, and whether there are any weak links.

Finally, if the person you are buying from is moving to a new-build property, press for their agreement to exchange contracts and complete regardless of whether or not the property is constructed on schedule. In winter months especially, weather conditions can hinder building work, leading to lengthy delays, which are not really your problem, and you could lose your buyer if you delay.

BUYING POSITIONS
Sellers will often accept an offer lower than the asking price if the buyer can complete the purchase quickly and easily, and this will depend on his or her buying position. Buyers fall into one of four categories, depending on their ability to proceed. In order of popularity, these are:

First-time buyer or cash purchaser
The buyer has nothing to sell, so is in an excellent bargaining position. Assuming his funding is in place, he can proceed with the purchase without delay.

Own property sold

The buyer's current property has been sold. This could mean that he has already moved out of his property into temporary accommodation (effectively making him a first-time buyer), or that contracts have been exchanged and he is just waiting for the formalities to be concluded. Either way, he has in effect disposed of his property and is in a position to buy quickly. This type of buyer can usually drive a hard bargain.

Sold subject to contract

This buyer has received an offer on his own property but has yet to exchange contracts, so there is still an element of doubt over whether the sale is secure. The length of chain he is involved in may be considered before any offer he makes is accepted.

On the market, but not yet sold

This buyer is in the same position as the person he is hoping to buy from. His buying status does not lend itself to bargaining over price, since it could take him longer to get an offer on his own property than for the seller to find another buyer. If this buyer's offer is accepted, the property will almost certainly remain actively for sale, in case someone in a better buying position comes along.

IN SUMMARY

- Know what the property is worth by researching comparable properties that have sold recently.
- Leave yourself room to increase your offer if your opening gambit is rejected.
- Bear in mind the cost of any necessary repairs.
- Make yourself an attractive buyer. Have your funding in place and your existing property sold (if applicable).

Chapter 3
SURVEYS AND VALUATIONS

WILL I NEED A SURVEY?

The short answer is undoubtedly 'yes', unless you are a surveyor yourself and you are not borrowing to finance your purchase. Apart from the fact that your lender will insist on one, it would be foolish to make such a large purchase without a second opinion on the property's condition and value.

All property purchases that rely on funding from banks or building societies have to be valued before the lender will part with any money. The property is the lender's security, so it needs to be sure that the property is sound, and worth at least the amount being borrowed, so that the loan can easily be recouped in the event of repossession.

The lender has a duty to itself (and arguably to the borrower) to ensure that the purchase is a sound investment. However, you should not assume that a lender's mortgage offer is any guarantee that the property is worth the purchase price; merely that it is worth the amount being lent on it.

Although it is the lender who insists on the valuation and/or survey, it is the borrower who pays for it.

MONEY-SAVING TIP

Shop around for the best price if you are having a survey or building report. It costs nothing to send out half a dozen emails to different surveyors, and you could easily save around £50 because prices vary between firms.

The surveyor has two main functions when preparing his report. Firstly, he gives his opinion on the value of the property, giving the lender and buyer an indication of how much the property could raise on disposal, should the need arise. Secondly, he checks that the property is in the condition it appears to be, bringing defects to the attention of the buyer and lender, although the level of detail and investigation will depend on the type of survey or valuation you opt for.

You should already have looked carefully at the property you want to buy, and taken note of any obvious faults, but an experienced surveyor ought to discover any major defects in the building that you might have missed. However, do not rely too heavily on a surveyor to protect your interests, especially if the inspection is a basic Valuation Report. This type of report, as the name suggests, is generally concerned with valuing the property from the lender's point of view, and will not unearth defects that might affect the living conditions or appearance of the property, which will be just as important to you. Even a comprehensive survey may not be conclusive. It will comment on serious decay or damage in the fabric of the building, but minor flaws might not be worthy of mention.

The extent of the surveyor's inspection is often limited by the access he is able to obtain, since fitted carpets and fitted or heavy furniture may be restrictive when it comes to inspecting floorboards and sections of wall. If the surveyor is unable to access certain areas of the property, his report will usually say so.

If you have a particular query regarding the property, you may be able to ask the surveyor to look at this specifically, although the flexibility of the information you receive will depend on the type of report commissioned, or to put it bluntly, how much you pay for it.

The value of a surveyor's report cannot be denied, and many buyers have been saved the expense and disruption of huge repairs because their surveyor pointed out defects which they themselves had not noticed. However, it is a mistake to assume that surveyors will report on every tiny defect in a property, and it is foolish to treat the report as insurance against any future defects. The surveyor can only comment on the condition of the property at the time of his inspection. He may, for example, report that the roof is in good condition, but can hardly be held responsible if a heavy storm some weeks later loosens several roof tiles, causing water damage.

Surveyors' reports generally carry a disclaimer to clarify exactly what the report covers (which is precious little in the case of a Valuation Report) and what it does not.

WHICH SURVEY TO CHOOSE?

Lenders will appoint a surveyor of their choice for a simple Valuation Report (see below), but if you decide to have a more detailed inspection, you will be able to choose the type of report, depending on the amount of information you hope to gain from it and the price you are willing to pay and, of course, you will be able to decide which surveyor to instruct, which will enable you to find the best price.

Valuation Report

A lender's Valuation Report is not a survey. It is primarily a valuation of the property to ensure that it provides adequate security for the loan (or mortgage) being secured on it. The value of the property must equal or exceed the amount the buyer is intending to borrow.

Lenders usually appoint their own surveyors for a simple valuation, so you have no say in who they use, although you will be paying for it.

The surveyor does not delve into the fabric of the building with this type of inspection. He will report on essential repairs which, if left uncorrected, would cause further damage to the property and hence affect its value, and will comment on specific aspects of the property's condition which have led to the valuation figure.

Defects mentioned tend to be only those that affect the value. Other defects, although they would involve repair costs, may not be mentioned.

Condition Report

This is the cheapest type of report, but it does not include a valuation, so you will need to pay for a lender's Valuation Report on top of this if you need to secure a loan for your purchase. A Condition Report is used primarily for modern houses that are in apparent good condition; it will highlight anything of major concern, but is not as extensive as a survey.

Home Buyer's Survey and Valuation Report (HSV)

This type of report will contain the surveyor's considered opinion regarding the value of the property at that time, and provides information on factors that might influence its future value. It is more in-depth than a Valuation Report, but only gives details of the property's general condition and any urgent matters needing attention.

It is prepared on a pre-printed form, so does not allow much flexibility, or room for comment on any particular queries you may have. It is not really suitable for properties older than 150 years, or those in need of renovation, and may not give you enough information if you are planning major alterations. It will tell you the value of the property, and the following points:

- The general condition of the property.
- Any major faults in accessible parts of the building that may affect the value.
- Any urgent problems that need further inspection by a specialist.
- Results of tests for damp in walls.
- Damage to timbers, including woodworm or rot.
- The condition of any damp-proofing, insulation and drainage (though drains are not tested).
- The estimated cost of rebuilding the property for insurance purposes.
- Anything that doesn't meet current building regulations.

MONEY-SAVING TIP
Check with your lender that the surveyor you are using is accepted by them for the purposes of the valuation, or they may insist on their own valuation as well, which you will pay for.

Building Survey

Sometimes referred to as a 'structural survey' or 'building report', this type of report is the most extensive. It is recommended for properties older than 150 years, any properties of unusual construction (such as timber framed), for listed buildings, and for those where alterations or renovations are planned.

The report is commissioned by the buyer and is usually more expensive than the HSV above, but the advantage is that it enables you to raise specific queries with the surveyor and ask him or her to report on areas of the property which concern you. In addition to points in the HSV above, a building survey will report on these points:

- The condition of all accessible parts of the building, including garages and outbuildings.
- Major and minor defects.
- An estimated cost of necessary repairs.
- Technical information regarding the construction of the property.
- Any recommended specialist reports or further inspections.

A building report will not necessarily include a valuation, which your lender will insist upon. Negotiate this with your surveyor before commissioning the report (they will often include it at no extra cost), and speak with your lender to make sure they will accept this, or you may have to pay for a lender's Valuation Report as well.

Surveys on leasehold properties

Unlike the survey on a freehold property, the report on a leasehold property will contain information about parts of the building not directly included in the purchase, because the condition of the whole building is relevant. As a leaseholder, you will be contributing to the maintenance and repair of areas outside your own four walls, and the general condition of the whole building affects the value of an individual flat.

USING THE RESULTS

The results of a valuation or survey may directly affect whether or not you choose to go ahead with the purchase, and at what price. Not only that, it also determines the amount your lender will be prepared to lend.

MONEY-SAVING TIP

Once you have a valuation and surveyor's report you are in a position to negotiate a price reduction on the property in view of any necessary repairs, or if the valuation figure is less than your offer.

A local surveyor will have a good knowledge of market prices and is often a better judge of property values than estate agents. Unlike the agents, he is not under pressure to meet the seller's aspirations, and gives a totally unbiased valuation. Be guided by the surveyor concerning value – it would be unwise to pay more for a property than the surveyor considers it is worth.

The results of a survey or valuation can break a property sale. Given this, the seller may wait for the results of your survey before going to the expense of paying for one on his purchase, in case his sale does not go ahead. This is an understandable practice, but obviously causes delay. It could also be an indication that the seller *expects* a surveyor to find something wrong with his property.

You should ensure that your solicitor is given a copy of any valuation or survey because there may be points in it which require clarification with the seller.

IN SUMMARY

- Decide on the type of survey you need, depending on the type of property you are buying, its condition and what you plan to do to it.
- Shop around for a good price.
- Speak to your surveyor about any specific aspects that are important to you.
- Make sure your solicitor receives a copy of your survey.
- If applicable, negotiate a reduction in the price of the property in consideration of any adverse reports.

Chapter 4
FINANCING A PURCHASE

WHAT IS A MORTGAGE?

Unless you are fortunate enough to have sufficient cash to buy a home outright, you will need to arrange some form of loan to fund the purchase of your property. Usually this is by way of a mortgage with a bank or building society.

A mortgage is a loan arranged specifically for the purchase of property. The lender, or *mortgagee* (the bank or building society) grants the borrower (the *mortgagor)* a sum of money. The borrower agrees to repay the loan and any incurred interest over a specified period (the *term*), which could be anything from, say, 10 to 35 years, during which time the lender holds the property as security, and the lender's interest is noted at the Land Registry.

This means that the lender can take possession of the property and sell it in order to settle the outstanding debt if the borrower fails to keep up the repayment schedule. You are allowed to occupy the property or to sell it at any time during the term of the mortgage, but if you sell the property, then the mortgage must be redeemed (paid off) before any balance of sale funds are given to you.

The property is the lender's security on the money loaned until the mortgage is repaid, but any increase in the value of the property belongs to you. Whilst the monthly repayment amounts may fluctuate as a result of changes to the prevailing interest rate (although not for fixed-rate mortgages), the capital amount owned cannot be increased by the lender.

The exception to this would be if you did not adhere to the conditions of the mortgage, for example by failing to insure the property or by not making the agreed repayments. In these circumstances, the lender may add costs to the amount outstanding.

If you sell the property before the end of the mortgage term, the proceeds of the sale are used to pay back the amount remaining on the loan, thereby redeeming the mortgage. If the property is sold for more than you borrowed, the extra money belongs to you, but if the property is sold for less than the outstanding loan, you will need to make up the difference to pay off the mortgage.

Sadly, many borrowers have found themselves in this position. Their property has dropped in value since they purchased it, and is now worth less than the loan secured on it. This distressing state of affairs has become known as 'negative equity' (see below).

If you decide to move home, you can often keep your existing mortgage, transferring it from one property to another, but you will need to check this with the lender. There will be some fees involved, for example a valuation of your new property, and the usual conveyancing costs.

FINDING THE RIGHT MORTGAGE

With so many institutions advertising mortgage lending, the choice of who to approach for funding can be baffling, and you will need to wade through a great deal of promotional material to get all the facts before making a final choice. It is crucial not to be rushed into the wrong type of mortgage for you, so take your time choosing the right one. This is one of the reasons it is better to start arranging your funding provisionally before you start looking for your new home. If you do it the other way round, the need to move quickly could force you into making a hasty decision.

THE DIRECT APPROACH

Lenders can be approached direct. You can request an appointment to speak with the mortgage adviser, who then explains in detail the various mortgages offered and any special deals they have available at the time. If you already have an account with a particular bank or building society you might prefer to keep all your financial affairs with one institution, but it does no harm to look around first, especially since lenders do not necessarily give preferential treatment to existing customers. If anything, it seems they are at pains to attract new customers, rather than working to retain their existing ones.

Be aware, though, that whichever lenders you approach, they can only tell you about their own products, which will not give you a good overview of the many mortgage deals available.

THE INTERNET

Internet money-saving sites will give you a quick guide to the best interest rates available at the time, but be aware that these change on a daily basis, so if you see a good offer you will need to move quickly to take advantage of it. The interest rate is not the only thing to look at here, and you will need to carefully assess all the facts and criteria of the product before going ahead with it. Not all lenders are featured all of the time.

You can also go onto the web sites of specific lenders to get information about the products they offer. But, if you see a deal that looks attractive, don't be tempted to click 'apply now' before you have spoken to the lender and found out everything about the mortgage. These sites are very useful as a general comparison guide, but always make sure that you get the full details before you proceed.

MONEY-SAVING TIP
Watch out for insurance top ups. It's usually far cheaper to arrange buildings and contents insurance yourself, rather than taking out a policy recommended by your lender or broker.

MORTGAGE BROKERS

Alternatively, you could approach a mortgage broker. The broker assesses your lending requirements and uses his knowledge of mortgages available at that time to find the best one for you. Brokers will often refer to their services as 'whole of market', indicating that they will check *all* mortgages available with a wide range of different lenders to find the best one for you, but some lenders have offers that are only available to direct customers and not via a broker.

Also, some lenders don't pay fees to brokers, so whilst 'whole of market' brokers should tell you about their products and include them in comparisons, they don't have to offer to implement these mortgages for you. At the moment, the main lenders who don't operate through brokers are Tesco Bank, Post Office, HSBC, First Direct, ING Direct and Yorkshire Building Society.

There's no doubt that mortgage brokers are helpful, but to get a complete picture of all mortgages you will have to do some research of your own.

> **MONEY-SAVING TIP**
> Some mortgage brokers charge a fee, and some don't. Make sure you are clear about charges before you ask a broker to do any work for you.

HOW MUCH CAN YOU BORROW?

Lenders are obliged to lend responsibly. This means they will not simply lend what you ask to borrow, but will carefully consider whether they think you can keep up the repayments now and in the future, for example after an initial discount period ends. They should base this consideration not only on your income, but also on your general expenditure and anything else that could make financial demands on you.

Lenders used to base their lending criteria solely on a borrower's salary. However, it has become more common for lenders to draw up an Affordability Assessment to calculate how much they are willing to lend. This is a more accurate assessment of what you can afford and aims to calculate your disposable income. To do this, they will consider the following information:

• Your total income, including extra money received by way of bonuses, overtime or commission. However, they may only take account of half of these extra amounts, because they are not guaranteed income.
• Any loans you already have, including credit cards.
• Household bills and living expenses.

They will also look at your credit history. If your credit report shows you have had difficulty keeping up with payments in the past, this may affect how much they will lend, or if they will lend at all. You can purchase a copy of your credit report from companies such as Experian or Equifax, from which you will see any negative listings that could cause a problem.

> **MONEY-SAVING TIP**
> Obtain a copy of your credit report before applying for your mortgage. Anything incorrect can then be removed before the lender applies for a copy, which could save you time, money and the embarrassment of refusal.

Even if you can easily afford to borrow the full purchase price, the lender will limit how much it will lend to a percentage of the property's value. This is called the loan-to-value ratio, or LTV. For example, if you were to borrow the entire purchase price, the LTV would be 100 per cent. If you borrow half, the LTV is 50 per cent.

At the time of writing, no lenders offer 100 per cent mortgages, although they used to. The range of mortgage deals on offer will be wider, and the interest rates more attractive, if you can lower the LTV by supplying a good sum of cash towards the purchase.

You will probably need a minimum deposit of 10 per cent of the purchase price, but to get a good deal on your mortgage, you'll ideally need 25 per cent, or more.

HOW MUCH SHOULD YOU BORROW?

Regardless of how much you *can* borrow, it is up to you to decide how much you should borrow, and that will depend on your income, expenditure and the monthly mortgage repayments.

Work out a simple income and expenditure budget. Bear in mind that a rise in interest rates will increase your repayments, and allow a buffer for this – don't allocate all your spare money to mortgage repayments at the outset. You will inevitably have maintenance and repair costs, so remember to include a float in the budget to cover these, too. An unexpected bill can put you in dire straits if your mortgage repayments are higher than you can comfortably afford. First-time buyers especially should be realistic in their budget calculations if they are not used to paying household bills.

MONEY-SAVING TIP
Prepare your budget and consult a mortgage lender or broker before starting to look for a property. That way you know how much you can afford and won't be tempted to look outside your price range.

When calculating expenditure, don't cheat – you must allow for *everything*. There are several online sites that enable you to enter income and expenditure and then calculate a workable budget. Include a miscellaneous amount to allow for all the cash that slips through your figures without you really knowing where it went.

Once you have calculated your expenditure, being honest and accurate, deduct this from your income. Use your current income, without assuming it will rise in the future. It may not, but your living costs will rise with inflation. If your income barely covers your outgoings, you do not have a financial safety net to cover any unexpected demands on your purse. You might be able to struggle through, but it is better to take out a smaller loan if you have any doubts at all.

MORTGAGE COSTS

Lenders charge a multitude of fees for taking out a mortgage. Here are some of them, and the amounts, although not all of them will apply to you:

MONEY-SAVING TIP

Make sure you know what fees you will be charged when choosing a lender – these vary enormously. Arrangement Fees and Early Redemption Charges especially could easily negate what appears to be a good deal.

Arrangement fee	Payment for setting up the mortgage. If you are declined or decide not to go ahead, you can normally get this fee refunded. Costs vary but can be up to 3.5 per cent of the amount borrowed.
Mortgage booking fee	Reserves your mortgage funds and/or covers administrative costs to process your mortgage. Not usually refundable. Cost varies, but is at least £100.
Mortgage account fee	Covers set up, maintenance and closing down your account. Cost around £200.
Valuation fee	To check that the property is of sufficient value to lend against. This is not the same as a survey. Cost is based on the value of the property.
Higher lending charge	Insurance cover for the lender if you are borrowing a high percentage of the value of the property (LTV, see page 44), to protect them if they repossess your home and sell it at a loss. They can still chase you for the shortfall, though. Cost varies
Own Buildings insurance fee	Administrative costs to check your policy is sound. Cost around £30.

Telegraphic transfer fee	Administrative cost to transfer funds direct to your solicitor on completion. Cost around £40.
Re-inspection fee	To check, for example, that agreed repairs have been carried out before funds are released. Cost £50–£100.
Early repayment charge	Penalty if you repay all or part of your mortgage earlier than the agreed term. Cost depends on length of term remaining.
Exit fee	Administrative charge to close your account, even if you are not repaying early. Cost varies.

MONEY-SAVING TIP

Some lenders will allow fees to be added to the mortgage, rather than settled up front. This may seem like a good idea at the time, but you will pay interest on the fees, making them even more expensive in the long run.

TYPES OF MORTGAGE

It is important to seek independent financial advice when taking out a mortgage. You will, after all, be paying it for many years, so you need to make sure it is the best arrangement for you, now and in the future. You can of course change your mortgage, and your lender, but this will incur fees (page 53). There are plenty of mortgages to choose from – here are the main points to consider for each one.

Interest only

With an interest-only mortgage you make monthly repayments for an agreed period, but you are only paying the interest on your loan.

Your monthly repayments will be lower than a repayment mortgage, but you are not reducing the amount you owe. Consequently, you will need to set up an investment or savings plan, in addition to your monthly interest payments, to enable you to pay off the loan at the end of the term. The risk here is that if your plan does not perform well, you may not have sufficient funds to repay the loan when required.

Bear in mind also that the total cost of this type of mortgage may be more expensive than a repayment arrangement, because you are paying interest on the whole amount of the loan for the entire term.

Repayment mortgage

With a repayment mortgage you make monthly repayments for the length of the mortgage term, until you have repaid the loan and the interest. Payments are calculated to stay the same throughout the term of the loan. Each month you will be reducing the amount you owe, although at the start of the mortgage most of what you pay will be interest, so if you repay the mortgage in the early years the amount outstanding will not have gone down by much.

Example – a £50,000 mortgage payable over 25 years

Year	Amount owed	Annual interest	Annual capital	Annual total
1	50,000.00	3,500.00	790.53	4,290.53
5	46,490.11	3,254.31	1,036.22	4,290.53
10	40,531.09	2,837.18	1,453.35	4,290.53
15	32,173.26	2,252.13	2,038.40	4,290.53
20	20,450.96	1,431.57	2,858.96	4,290.53
25	4,009.84	280.69	4,009.84	4,290.53

It's a fairly simple system to understand, and as long as you keep up your repayments, you will have repaid your loan in full at the end of the term.

Standard Variable Rate (SVR)

Your monthly payments will go up or down, in line with the lender's standard interest rate. This rate is determined by the individual lender and is not linked directly to the Bank of England's base rate, although you can expect the Bank of England's base rate to impact on your lender's interest rate – increasing or decreasing accordingly. Lenders can also normally change their standard variable rate even if the base rate has not moved.

There are often incentives offered with this type of mortgage, such as Cash Back, giving you an additional lump sum that is not part of the loan. As with any incentive, the object is to tie you in to the mortgage long term, so if you repay the loan early or change lender, you will be penalized and effectively have to pay back the incentive.

Discounted rate

The rate of interest you pay at the beginning of the loan will be 'discounted' to a lower rate. After a fixed period, you will move to another rate, usually the lender's standard variable rate, for the rest of the term. There will be penalties if you repay this type of mortgage early.

Tracker

The rate of interest is linked to the Bank of England base rate, although it is not necessarily the same rate. If the Bank of England's base rate goes up or down, the interest rate you pay will rise or fall at the same rate.

Fixed rate

The rate of interest you pay will stay the same for a fixed period at the start of the term, regardless of fluctuations in the lender's standard variable rate. This enables you to know exactly what your monthly payments will be for the term of the fixed rate. Once that term expires, you will usually move to the lender's standard variable rate. If you pay off your mortgage early, there will be penalties.

Capped
With a capped rate you pay a variable interest rate, but there is a ceiling, so your payments won't go above a certain amount for a set period. This enables you to budget because you know your repayments will not go above a set limit, regardless of general interest rate rises. Some deals also include a 'collar', which is the lowest rate of interest you will pay.

Flexible
A flexible mortgage gives you some scope to change your monthly repayments to suit your ability to pay. It is a useful type of mortgage if you have a variable income, or if you expect your income to change over the term of the loan. If you are not likely to use the features of this type of mortgage, it will not be good value for money. Some of the flexible features are:

- **Overpayments** You can increase the amount you pay each month, or pay off a lump sum. If you pay off a chunk of the loan, you will reduce the amount of your monthly repayments, because you will owe less. If you increase the amount you pay each month, you will pay off the loan quicker. Some lenders allow you to do both.
- **Underpayments and payment holidays** You are able to reduce your normal monthly payment for a specified period (say six to twelve months). You may even be able to stop making payments altogether (a payment holiday). This could be useful if your income is reduced or if, for example, you lose your job.
- **Draw down** This allows you to borrow more money, up to a maximum level, without having to go through the approval process again with the lender. Alternatively, you may be able to 'borrow back' against earlier overpayments if you have made any.

Offset

With an offset mortgage, your main current account and/or savings account are linked to your mortgage account. The amount of your mortgage is reduced each month by the amount in these accounts. If your current account and savings balances go up, you pay less on your mortgage. As they go down, you pay more. If you have a healthy amount of savings, this type of mortgage could be right for you, although the interest rates are often higher than the lender's standard variable rate.

Current account

Like the offset mortgage, a current account mortgage uses the balance of your savings to reduce the amount of your mortgage. The difference is that, rather than your mortgage and current account being separate pots of money, they are usually combined into one account. This means that the account acts like one big overdraft, and you reduce the amount of the 'overdraft' whenever you top up your savings. This could be the right mortgage for you if you have a lot of savings, and need the flexibility to make overpayments or underpayments. However, the interest rate is likely to be higher than many other mortgages.

MONEY-SAVING TIP

Look for the APR figure when choosing a mortgage. This will tell you the overall cost and not just the interest rate. A good mortgage broker will be able to tell you the total cost of borrowing during the deal.

Staged lending or Self build

If you are buying a plot of land to build on, you can take out a mortgage on the land, but not on the cost of building the property.

This is because until the building is up, there is nothing to secure the loan on. However, you may be able to arrange a 'staged loan', which would release additional funds to you as the building work progresses.

This type of lending may also be used if you buy a property that needs renovating. Some funds will be released to buy the building in its current state, then further funding is released as the renovations progress and the property increases in value.

THE MORTGAGE OFFER

Once your mortgage application is approved and the property has been inspected by a surveyor, the lender will issue a formal mortgage offer: written confirmation of the amount the lender is willing to lend, and details of the loan.

The mortgage offer is usually received a few days after the surveyor submits the valuation report or survey to the lender, unless there is cause for further investigation, for example if the surveyor suggests obtaining a specialist report on a specific aspect of the property. The time taken between application and formal offer is usually around three weeks, but it can take up to eight, depending on the lender.

Mortgage offers have an expiry date. If your offer expires before you complete your property purchase, you may have to apply all over again and may not get the same terms as the original offer. If you suspect your mortgage offer may expire before you can complete, speak to the lender and ask for an extension.

MONEY-SAVING TIP

Obtaining a Mortgage in Principle (MIP) from your lender will give you an advantage when you find a house you want to buy. It shows that your finance is in place and improves your bargaining status.

SECOND MORTGAGES

A second mortgage is, as the name suggests, a further loan secured on a property. The reason for the loan is usually irrelevant. It doesn't matter to the lender whether you want to fund an extension to the property or your child's university costs, but there must be enough equity in the property to cover the second and first mortgages combined.

If the second mortgage is taken out with a different lender from the first mortgage, you will need the original lender's approval. The lender of the second mortgage will also have to be told that the property is already mortgaged. The process of applying for a second mortgage is much the same as obtaining any mortgage – the property will need to be valued again and you will need to produce evidence of your income. You will incur fees from the lender, and solicitors' fees to register the second charge with the Land Registry.

REMORTGAGING

You can choose to swap to a different mortgage at any time – not just when moving house – and may either stay with the same lender or move your mortgage to a different lender. This is referred to as remortgaging.

Depending on your financial circumstances, there can be some sound financial reasons for doing this.

- Extending the term of the loan. This will reduce the amount of your monthly repayments, which may be useful if you are struggling to keep up with them.
- Reduce the term of the loan. For example, if your salary increases and you are able to make higher monthly repayments and so pay off your mortgage more quickly.
- Increase the mortgage amount, perhaps to release funds to pay off other more expensive debts, such as credit cards. This is called 'debt consolidation'. While this may make your overall debts easier

to manage and the interest rates lower, think carefully before turning unsecured debts into debt secured against your home.

- Reduce the mortgage amount. For example, if you have a lump sum available, you could then either make smaller monthly repayments over the same term, or reduce the term and pay off the mortgage more quickly
- Take advantage of a lower rate of interest on a different product.

> **MONEY-SAVING TIP**
> Possibly the best way to save money is to get a better lending rate. Just a 1 per cent drop on the interest you are paying will save you thousands of pounds in the long run.

You will need to bear in mind any early repayment charges in your calculations, as they can be very high (refer to your Mortgage Offer to see if these apply to you). Also, if your current mortgage had financial incentives like Cash Back or 'fees paid', you may have to pay these back.

In addition, there will be fees payable to the new lender and legal fees, so these costs need to be factored in too, although some lenders will pay them as part of their mortgage deal.

TAX

Tax, it seems, is unavoidable. Thankfully, unless you are a property investor or a landlord, the only time you will pay property tax is when you buy a property and possibly, if you own more than one, when you sell it.

STAMP DUTY LAND TAX (SDLT)

Stamp Duty is payable on any property purchased for more than £125,000. The duty is calculated as a percentage of the whole purchase price, so the SDLT payable on a property purchased for £200,000 would be 1 per cent of £200,000, not 1 per cent of the amount over the £125,000 nil-rate threshold. The Stamp Duty rate changes according to the price of the property.

£0 to £125,000	0%
£125,001 to £250,000	1%
£250,001 to £500,000	3%
£500,001 to £1 million	4%
Over £1 million to £2 million	5%
Over £2 million	7%

For leasehold properties, SDLT is payable on both the purchase price (in the same way as for freehold properties), and also on the annual rent if it is more than just a peppercorn rent.

Your solicitor will complete the SDLT return form for you, and he or she will be well versed in the rates payable. However, if you have any doubt about how much you should be paying, the HM Revenue & Customs website has all the information you need and a handy calculator.

CAPITAL GAINS TAX

When an asset such as property or land is sold for more than the price at which it was purchased, the 'gain' (or profit) is liable to Capital Gains Tax. If the property is your main or only residence, this tax will not apply to you, because you qualify for an exemption called Private Residence Relief (PRR). However, if you are buying an additional property or land, perhaps as an investment or second home, you will be liable to pay Capital Gains Tax on any profit made on disposal of that property. For a property to qualify for PRR, it must be your only home or main residence, and you must have used it as your home and for no other purpose. You do not have to claim PRR – it is given automatically.

There are fairly complicated rules regarding Capital Gains Tax where a property is used for business purposes or is let out, for example. Contact HM Revenue & Customs if you have any doubts about your liability.

MORTGAGE CRISIS

'Your home is at risk if you do not keep up the repayments on your mortgage or other loan secured on it.'

These sobering words appear in one form or another on all advertisements for mortgages, warning potential borrowers that they could lose their home if they fall behind with repayments. The statement might make you think twice about your responsibilities when taking on a mortgage, which is a good thing, but since financial difficulties are usually unintentional and unpredictable, as a warning it's pretty useless.

The vast majority of homeowners never experience problems repaying a mortgage, so it would be wrong to paint a picture of doom and gloom. However, you cannot ignore the statistics of more than 36,000 repossessions in 2011, so it is sensible to give some thought to what you would do if you found yourself in mortgage crisis.

MONEY-SAVING TIP

Can you reduce your mortgage with spare savings? Many lenders allow you to repay up to 10 per cent of the loan value without penalty. It's likely you will be paying more interest on your loan than you will be getting on your savings, so this could be a better use of your money if you don't need access to your savings, but do check for penalty payments on your mortgage first.

The sad fact is that carefully planned budgets and cautious borrowings are sometimes not enough to guard against financial crisis. Jobs for life are a thing of the past, and redundancy and divorce are commonplace. Consequently, many people are unable to make their monthly mortgage repayments because of reduced circumstances through no fault of their own.

If you cannot afford to pay your mortgage it can seem an insurmountable problem, but there is help at hand if you know where to look for it, and it is vitally important that you seek this help as soon as possible.

The first rule is to speak to your lenders. Many have telephone helplines and staff who have been specifically trained to deal with customers in this predicament. What you should *not* do is let the problem escalate out of hand before seeking help. By consulting with your lender, you may be able to:

• Reduce your monthly payments
• Make interest-only payments for a while
• Extend the term of your loan

Do not be pressured into agreeing to make higher payments than you can afford just to satisfy the lender. This is not a long term solution. If you cannot keep up these new repayments, you will be in an even worse position, because in effect you will be defaulting for a second time.

Ultimately, the arrears will have to be paid one way or another, sometimes by adding them to the outstanding loan or by an arrangement of supplementary payments, but in the vast majority of cases, an agreement can be made between you and your lender without losing your home.

MONEY-SAVING TIP

The Citizens Advice Bureau is a wonderful source of free and independent information. If they cannot help, they will point you in the direction of someone who can.

There are plenty of agencies out there specifically set up to help the growing number of people in all kinds of debt situations, from mortgage arrears to business bankruptcy. People like the Step Change Debt Charity, for example, offer free and unbiased advice. Not all debt management is free, though, so make sure you are clear about any charges.

DEFAULT AND REPOSSESSION

When you take out a mortgage, your main obligation is to repay the sum borrowed, plus any interest, over the period specified. If you fail to meet this obligation you are in breach of the mortgage contract, and the lender can apply for possession of the mortgaged property in order to sell it and recoup the outstanding debt.

Most lenders are keen to avoid repossession and only take such drastic action as a last resort. They would far rather come to some arrangement to allow you to retain your home. It is in their interest as well as yours to avoid repossession, and they will usually agree to defer any action if you demonstrate a willingness to make regular payments, albeit less than the usual repayment amount.

If you do not speak to your lender to sort out a solution between you, they have little recourse but to go down the route of repossession. Different lenders have different procedures, but as a guide, this is what would happen:

1. **You miss a payment**

   Lender writes to bring the missed payment to your attention.

2. **You do nothing and miss more payments**

   Lender informs you that solicitors are being instructed to recover the debt. The lender must inform you that payments are late – this is referred to as a Notice of Default.

3. **You do nothing**

   Lender's solicitor writes to you, threatening Court action.

4. **You still do nothing**

   Solicitors start County Court Repossession proceedings. The court advises you of the hearing date.

5. **You attend Court**

   Either: The court suspends the Order of Repossession if you present a plan of how you propose to pay the lender, usually by monthly instalments, including a set amount towards the arrears. Or: If you cannot do this, the court will pass an Order of Repossession and propose a date for repossession of the property.

6. **Eviction**

   The lender obtains a bailiff's warrant from the court. Bailiffs give you final notice and set a date for eviction.

This is not a fast process, and the period of time between the first missed payment and eviction can be around a year. The good thing is that it can usually be avoided by agreeing a payment schedule with the lender, but many borrowers allow the situation to get out of hand by missing more and more payments in the hope that they will be able to put matters right the next month, or the next.

Do not despair if you miss a few payments. So long as, at any time from the first missed payment to the court hearing, you sort out a payment schedule to the satisfaction of the lender, or repay the arrears, eviction proceedings will usually be halted.

If the lender is opposed to your payment schedule and still takes you to court, the court may well decide in your favour and allow you to make the payments you have suggested, and suspend an

Order of Repossession. Make sure the payment schedule you propose is realistically within your means, because repossession is only suspended. If you fail to keep up the new payments the lender can enforce your eviction from the property without going back to court.

A common myth is that you can hand the keys over to the lender and walk away from the debt. Not so. The property will be disposed of at auction or estate sale, and probably won't sell for the best price. If the price achieved does not cover what you owe, the lender can still pursue you for the amount outstanding.

Communication is the key. If you have a problem making repayments, or if you anticipate a problem, speak to your lender straight away. They are far more likely to be helpful if you show yourself to be sensible enough to tackle the problem head on, rather than ignore it.

NEGATIVE EQUITY

Sadly, when looking at mortgages it is necessary to say a word or two about negative equity – what it is, and why it has become so common.

Home ownership is the norm nowadays, and most people aspire to owning their own home, believing the value of it will increase over the years. However, in the last two decades the property market has seen some dramatic ups and downs, and while some people have made money on property, a great many have lost out.

The lucky ones found that the home they bought rose in value, giving them increased 'equity' in the property – the value of the property less any mortgage or loan secured against it. The reverse is the case with negative equity – the property decreases in value, leaving the owners with a bigger loan than the property is worth.

So what can you do if you find yourself in this position? You could sell the property. Of course, the sale proceeds will not cover the outstanding mortgage, so you will need to consult your lender before you do this to agree how you propose to pay off the outstanding amount. Bear in mind that you will incur fees in the sale – estate agents, and solicitors, for a start – and you will have nowhere to live.

As an alternative, you may be able to sell your existing property and transfer the mortgage (with negative equity) to a new property. The idea behind this is that you buy a cheaper property, reducing the amount of the mortgage, thereby freeing up funds to repay the shortfall over a period of time. There will, however, be both selling and buying costs involved in this.

Or you could stay put. Negative equity is only really a problem if you want to remortgage or sell your home, or if the market looks set to continue falling. If the market is level, the sensible option would be to stay where you are and hope that the value will increase in time to move back above the level of your loan. Thankfully, history shows this is usually the case.

IN SUMMARY

- Research the mortgage market as much as possible.
- Speak to several different brokers for their opinion and to gather information.
- Check the various brokers' fees before you instruct one.
- Don't borrow more than you need or want to.
- Be honest with yourself when calculating how much you can afford to borrow.
- Check your Mortgage Offer to make sure you are happy with it before you accept it. If you don't understand anything, ask.
- Make sure your lender has everything required of you. Don't leave it till the last minute to find out there is something outstanding, which could hold up the entire buying process.
- Be aware of added costs involved in setting up a mortgage.
- If you have any problems making monthly payments, speak to the lender straight away.

Chapter 5
LEASEHOLD PROPERTY

WHAT IS A LEASE?

Simply put, a lease is a contract granting the right to occupy a property for a specific length of time, usually in return for rent. In the case of buying a leasehold residential property, the rent is termed 'ground rent'. The person who buys the lease (the *lessee*) temporarily owns the property for the length of time stipulated in the lease.

The lease plan will show exactly what is included in the leasehold premises, for example a designated car-parking space, as well as the actual rooms, and will also show any rights of way over common areas such as communal halls.

Unlike the purchase of a freehold, where the buyer is the absolute owner and can do more or less what he wants with the property, a lessee must comply with any restrictions (or covenants) written into the lease, which limit what he can do on, or to, the premises. If you buy a lease, you need to be sure these covenants are reasonable and agreeable to you. Generally, flats are leasehold and houses are freehold, but there are exceptions.

Buying a lease is not like renting, although lessees are sometimes referred to as tenants. Rental tenants and leasehold tenants both enter into an agreement that grants occupation for a specific length of time and for an agreed amount of rent, but the similarity ends there. A rental agreement is usually short term, say six months. Payment for occupation is in the form of routinely paid rent (weekly or monthly), and this is usually the only payment the landlord receives. With a lease, however, the length of the term is for many years, and the lessee pays a one-off payment for the right of occupation (the purchase price) in addition to a 'ground rent', which will be nominal.

Estate-agency written details should not be relied on to give a full picture of what you will be buying. Whereas with a freehold property what you see is what you get, in the case of a leasehold property it is easy to be misled when viewing it. You may, for example, be most impressed with the grounds surrounding a block of flats you view, but may later discover that access to the grounds is not included in the lease. Or perhaps the parking space you use during a viewing does indeed belong to the block, but not to the particular flat you are thinking of buying.

MONEY-SAVING TIP

Make sure your conveyancing quote is a fixed fee and cannot be increased if the process takes longer than anticipated, which often happens with leasehold transfers.

LANDLORDS AND LESSEES

The freeholder (or landlord) of a leasehold property owns the land on which the property is built, even though for the term of the lease the leaseholder is the registered proprietor of the premises. The landlord can sell his freehold interest to a third party, who then becomes the new landlord. A new landlord would give notice to the lessees of a change of ownership, and service charges or other fees would then be paid to him. A change of landlord should go largely unnoticed by the lessees because the new landlord must operate within the covenants of the leases already granted, although the new landlord may be better or worse at fulfilling his obligations, and more or less amendable should a problem arise.

If you are buying a leasehold property, you either buy it from the current lessee, or directly from the freeholder; for example a flat in a newly built block where a new lease is being created. All leases run for a specified period of time, which means the term of the lease diminishes each year. If a lease is left to run out, the premises eventually revert to the landlord's ownership.

It may be possible to extend the lease period by negotiation with the freeholder. If you have lived in the property for more than two years and the original lease term was more than 21 years, you have a right to extend the lease for up to 90 years. There will be costs involved, but a solicitor will be able to tell you if you qualify for this type of extension. Some leases contain a clause giving the lessee the opportunity to renew the lease before it expires.

WHAT YOU NEED TO KNOW

When you are buying a leasehold property, your solicitor will ask the seller's solicitor for a lot of information about the premises, the lease and the management of the building in which the premises are located. He will usually ask for the following information, and should send you a list of his enquiries and the resulting replies.

- The name, address and telephone number of the Landlord or Management Agents.
- Any consents required for assignment of the lease (passing the lease from the seller to you).
- Ground rent payments for the last three years.
- Service Charge receipts for the last three years.
- Management accounts for the last three years.
- Copy buildings insurance together with up-to-date policy schedule.
- The Articles of Association and Memorandum of the management company (if there is one), and a copy of the share certificate.
- Details of any Notice Fees payable.
- Whether a Deed of Covenant or License to Assign are required.
- The date on which the ground rent and basic maintenance is paid, and the sum paid per annum.
- How many flats there are in the building.
- How many floors there are in the building.
- Whether all the flats are let on a similar form of lease.
- Details of any disputes between the existing lessee and the landlords and/or owners or occupiers of any other units within the building.
- When the exterior and common parts were last redecorated.
- Whether there are any major items of maintenance expenditure envisaged within the short to medium term.
- Whether there have been any alterations to the building since the lease was granted.
- Whether or not any other charges are to be made independently of the maintenance charge.
- Whether there are any reserve funds, and if so what proportion is attributed to the seller, and if the reserve is considered adequate?
- A copy of the up-to-date Asbestos and Fire Safety Risk Assessment in relation to the common parts of the building pursuant to the Regulatory Reform (Fire Safety) Order 2005.

These are standard enquiries that would apply to most leasehold properties, but if there is anything specific you want to know, ask you solicitor to enquire about it. The seller will also be asked to complete the usual information forms mentioned in the Conveyancing section, Chapter 8.

RESTRICTIONS AND COVENANTS

Into every lease are written certain restrictions and stipulations, which the landlord and lessee both agree to abide by when entering into the lease agreement. Usually the heavier burden of restrictions falls on the lessee (things you must NOT do on or to the premises), while the more onerous stipulations apply to the landlord (he MUST repair and maintain the building, for example). Once a restriction or stipulation has been included in the lease, it is generally there for the duration.

Covenants are also included. These are formal promises, or undertakings, to do or refrain from doing certain things, and let you know what you will be agreeing to if you buy the lease. They usually include payment of rent and upkeep of the premises, and may state for example that the lessee is not permitted to alter the premises, carry on a business there or keep pets.

Whilst the covenants may seem restrictive, they act in a positive way to protect the resale value of the lease by aiming to ensure that the building as a whole does not deteriorate. This is important because the overall appearance of a block of flats reflects on the value and saleability of each flat.

The landlord promises to allow the tenant 'quiet enjoyment' of the premises and to abide by the stipulations and restrictions imposed on him, for example to repair, maintain and insure the building.

Landlords and tenants have enforceable power over each other to ensure the covenants are complied with, but one tenant does not have power over another. Restraining a tenant from committing an act which is in breach of the covenant (perhaps he is causing a nuisance to other tenants) is a matter for the courts by way of an injunction brought by the landlord or the management company. The court will then order the offender to stop doing whatever it is they are doing which is contrary to the terms of the covenants.

OBLIGATIONS OF THE LANDLORD

As well as specific covenants, there are some obligations that landlords are forced to adhere to, whether or not they are specifically mentioned in the lease. These are general rules, which are automatically 'implied' when a landlord and lessee enter into their relationship, and are an attempt to ensure that the lessee is not subjected to unreasonable negligent acts by the landlord.

Common areas

Regarding common parts of the building in which a flat is situated and which are owned by the landlord (for example the stairway), the landlord is obliged to ensure that they are kept in reasonable condition. The landlord is liable to the lessee for any injury suffered as a result of the area being unsafe if he is in breach of his duty of care.

Safety

The lessee is protected against a negligent landlord who fails to uphold his responsibilities and obligations if such negligence results in damage. Furthermore, the landlord is obliged to ensure that those parts of the building that are in his control are safe for use by the lessees, their visitors and anyone else who might reasonably be expected to use them (the postman, for example). However, generally it is the responsibility of the lessee to ensure that the leased premises are safe, and a person suffering injury in the flat itself (as opposed to the common areas held by the landlord) will direct a complaint or claim for compensation against the holder of the lease.

Quiet enjoyment

Lessees have the basic right to 'quiet enjoyment' of the leased premises. 'Quiet enjoyment' is not concerned with noise (which is classed as nuisance) but means that the tenant must be free to live in his home without unnecessary interference, which could give rise to distress or inconvenience. This could include damage to the lessee's premises as a result of a fault in the building where the landlord has failed to uphold his obligation to repair and maintain. In this case, because of the damage to the premises, the lessee's enjoyment of them has been affected. 'Enjoyment' and 'interference' have to be reasonable, and are not to be taken as the effect on a person of unusual sensitivity.

Nuisance

The lessee has the right to sue the landlord in cases of nuisance. This could happen when, for example, the landlord fails in his responsibility to maintain refuse chutes which then become foul smelling and a nuisance to the lessees. Recourse against a landlord who causes nuisance can also be taken up with the Environmental Health Department of the local authority. The department will investigate anything that is deemed to be a danger to health, and if the landlord is found to be at fault, will specify to him the necessary action to rectify the situation.

The landlord is not, however, responsible to each of the lessees for the nuisance of any of the others. The landlord may be willing to act as mediator between lessees in the interests of harmony, and may be an aggrieved lessee's best first approach, but if the landlord is unable or unwilling to resolve a dispute between lessees, there may be no alternative but to apply to the courts for an action against the offender's behaviour.

UNDERSTANDING THE TERMS OF YOUR LEASE

You need to know everything you can about a lease and its covenants, before you consider buying the associated property. The selling agents rarely have detailed information about the lease as part of their sale details, and information provided by them should not be taken as conclusive or complete. Your solicitor is a far better source of factual information, since he will be supplied with a copy of the lease by the seller's solicitor, and he will make enquiries on practical matters, such as services provided and related charges, insurance and boundaries, as part of the conveyancing process.

Since leases are lengthy and complicated documents that use jargon unfamiliar to most of us, it is helpful if your solicitor prepares a summary of the lease in simple terms so that you can understand the key points. For example:

- How much are the service charges?
- Under what circumstances does the landlord have the right to enter the premises?
- What repairing obligations, if any, apply to you?
- What repairing obligations apply to the landlord?
- What restrictions are there concerning alterations or improvements to the premises?
- Are you allowed a satellite dish?
- Where are the waste bins?
- Have there been any noise or nuisance issues between other flat owners?

BREACH OF COVENANT

In theory, by entering into a lease, both parties willingly agree to abide by the covenants contained in it, and both live happily ever after. But what happens if one or other strays from their agreement and becomes in breach of a covenant? A covenant is only of any use if the party who is failing to abide by it can be forced to adhere to it. What could you do, for example, if the landlord is failing in his responsibility to periodically redecorate the exterior of the building?

Firstly, you would need to be sure that the landlord really is in breach. This is no point complaining that the building is in need of decorating if the landlord is not obliged to carry out the work for another year. If the work is overdue, the first stage of action would be to write to the landlord or managing agent, pointing out the problem and asking when the work is likely to be put into effect. If this approach does not work, you may have to take the matter further through a court order, forcing the landlord to stand by his obligations, but the cost, complexities and potential animosity resulting from legal action must make the courts a last resort.

If the landlord is obliged to repair the building, the courts have the power to order the landlord to make repairs agreed to in the terms of the lease. Alternatively, as a tenant you could arrange for the repairs to be done yourself and then withhold further payments of service charge until you have been reimbursed for your outlay. Do speak to your solicitor before you do this, though, to ensure that you are acting within your rights according to the lease, because if you withhold rent your landlord could seek to forfeit the lease for non-payment of rent. In this case, two wrongs do not make a right.

If you do arrange to have repairs carried out, you must take reasonable measures to ensure the costs are not excessive, by obtaining at least two estimates and employing the contractor who submits the lower one – and you must advise the landlord of your intentions *before* carrying out the work.

SERVICE CHARGES

As well as the ground rent, as a lessee you will usually have to pay a service charge, typically an annual payment, which will recompense the landlord for his financial outlay in supplying certain services. If you and the other lessess enjoy such services as lifts, these must be maintained, and common areas like entrance halls need to be cleaned and well lit. The cost of providing these services is recouped by the landlord by way of a service charge 'contribution' made by each lessee.

Also covered by the service charge will be the general repair and maintenance of the building, insurance and the landlord's costs in relation to administration and professional fees incurred in the business of overseeing the building.

As a potential buyer of a lease, you need full details of the service charge, as this is an on-going payment and can be costly. Not only do you need to know how much the service charge is, but also exactly what services are covered by the payment and how the charges are calculated between the lessees. In some cases, the apportionment of costs may not be equally split, and those whose property is on the ground floor, for example, may have a lower service charge than those who make use of the lift.

Similarly, tenants of the larger flats in a block may pay a higher service charge than those in smaller flats, the apportionment being based on floor space or rateable value.

Your solicitor will ask the seller to provide annual accounts from the management company and details of previous service charge bills (and receipts) to get an idea of what they have been for the last few years.

MONEY-SAVING TIP

Ask your solicitor to enquire if there are any major repairs or maintenance plans in the near future. If there are, the service charge for that year could be high. You may be able to negotiate a reduction in the purchase price to allow for this.

MAINTENANCE COSTS

Usually the lease stipulates a year-end accounting date, at which time the landlord or management company will prepare details of annual costs up to that date, and circulate a copy to lessees. The lessees will usually be expected to make estimated payments during the annual period. At the end of the period, if the estimated charges have fallen short of actual costs, they will receive a demand for a further payment to make up the difference. If the estimate was high, resulting in an excess of funds, the excess is usually held against the next year's service charge.

In an attempt to budget for major expenses anticipated in future years, the landlord may set up a 'sinking fund', which enables costs to be spread out and avoids a situation where lessees would need to make a particularly large service-charge payment in any one year. If the person you are buying from has an amount held in his name 'on credit' in the sinking fund, you may be asked to reimburse him this amount when you complete the purchase.

FORFEITURE OF THE LEASE

If you fail to pay rent (regardless that the amount on a long lease is likely to be nominal), the action open to the landlord is to repossess the premises and effectively cancel the lease. He can only do this if there is a covenant in the lease which stipulates that he may do so. Non-payment of rent does not automatically end the lease – indeed some ground rents are so small that the landlord does not bother to collect them (although they remain outstanding, since it is the obligation of the lessee to pay, and not the landlord's obligation to collect), but the landlord has the option of taking severance action if he wishes.

The landlord may also enforce forfeiture if you are in breach of other terms of the lease, but can only do so after you have been given the opportunity to mend your ways and pay compensation if applicable. In other words, he cannot intentionally allow you to do something that is contrary to your obligations in order to trap you.

The process of the courts in such situations follows a set procedure controlled by particular Acts and timescales, usually giving the tenant ample chance to remedy the problem before it gets out of hand and the lease is terminated. However, the prospect should not be viewed flippantly: the terms of a lease are legally binding and you should not enter into anything that you are not happy to abide by.

IN SUMMARY

- Make sure you are comfortable owning a leasehold property and all that entails.
- Understand your obligations and the restrictions imposed by the lease.
- Be clear on the cost of service charges, ground rent and future maintenance requirements.
- Make sure you have details of the landlord or managing agents so that you can contact them if necessary.

Chapter 6
BUYING A NEWLY BUILT HOME

WHY CHOOSE A NEW BUILD?

New-home sites seem to be popping up all over the place, so there is bound to be one somewhere near you or in your search area. Buying a brand new house or flat has its advantages, and these can be very compelling when you are looking to buy a property.

• You can often gain access before completion, at the builder's discretion, which is very useful for arranging carpet fitting and other preparations before actually moving in.

- For first-time buyers especially, the process of buying a newly built home is considerably less complicated than getting involved in a chain.
- The very newness of a freshly built home is extremely appealing. It is a clean page, ready to be stamped with your own personality. The decoration is usually acceptable, so there is no need to spend every foreseeable weekend stripping off old wallpaper.
- The property is ready to move into, so you don't need to budget for alterations.
- New homes come with a 10-year warranty against structural defects (see NHBC below).
- New homes are far more energy efficient than older houses, so running costs are lower.

MONEY-SAVING TIP

A costly Building Survey is not necessary for a new home, because the standard 10-year building warranty covers future problems. A Homebuyer's Survey and Valuation Report should be enough (see Surveys and Valuations pages 31 and 34).

However, there can be drawbacks to a brand-new home, and one of the most obvious is that building work can be delayed for all sorts of reasons. This is particularly tricky if you are selling your current home before buying a new one. Your buyer will not want to wait indefinitely for your new home to be finished, so you may be forced to complete on your sale before you have somewhere to move to.

Do bear in mind that the newness doesn't last. Think of it like buying a brand-new car. As soon as you drive it out of the showroom it becomes second hand and starts to devalue. Pretty soon a brand-new home becomes 'second hand', and any premium you paid for that newness will be lost.

OFFERS AND INCENTIVES

Builders come up with all sorts of tempting offers to sell their new properties, but you need to be a bit cynical here. After all, rarely do you get something for nothing. If you pay more than necessary for the property to take advantage of a financial incentive, the incentive is effectively 'bought' along with the property itself. The cost of it will therefore be lumped in with your loan and incurs interest throughout the term of your mortgage.

The first two incentives listed below involve some sort of financial handout, but in most cases what is given with one hand is taken away with the other. These offers are particularly appealing to buyers who don't have much ready cash. First-time buyers especially find incentives useful, since having struggled to fund a deposit they have little left over for carpets, furniture and other expenses. Here are some offers explained.

Cash Back

The buyer receives a one-off sum of money from the builder on completion of the purchase. Buyers are attracted to this because it gives them extra cash for the inevitable expenses of moving home, although in reality the Cash Back sum is almost certainly built into the purchase price.

Fees paid

The builder agrees to pay some of the buyer's purchasing expenses (usually legal costs or survey fees) up to a maximum amount. The buyer may have to pay these fees initially, and then apply for a refund. Again, the cost of this incentive will be built into the purchase price.

Part exchange

This can be a very helpful arrangement if you don't want to get involved in a chain, or are having difficulty selling your present property. Simply put, the builder buys your property, which enables you to buy his. Builders often offer around 5 per cent less than the market value on the property they are buying, but some now offer a full market value based on three valuations. As long as you are happy with the price being asked for the new house and are getting a good price for your existing property, this can be a very convenient and quick transaction.

MONEY-SAVING TIP

Do your sums. It's often better to negotiate a good purchase price than take advantage of incentives.

VISITING A NEW-HOME SITE

Builders of new homes often have a site office, show-home and full-time sales staff on site, so it is not always necessary to make an appointment to view the properties – you can just turn up. Builders who do not have site offices instruct estate agents to manage sales, so viewings by appointment are arranged through the agency in the usual way.

MONEY-SAVING TIP

Staff employed on site are expert sales people with targets to meet. Don't be talked into spending more than you intend, or into making a hasty purchase.

At the sales office or estate agency, you will be able to see a plan of the site, which is particularly useful if the site is in its early stages. These plans enable you to view the site as a whole, to see how crowded it will be and where access roads and any green spaces will be located. It can be difficult to imagine the finished site if construction work is still under way, so do take time to look at the plan carefully.

However, be aware that these plans are not always to scale, and certainly the 'artist's impression' of what the site will eventually look like is just that – an impression, and often a rosy one at that.

Properties of differing styles will be identified by name or colour on the plan, so even if the site is nowhere near completion, you can see where the building of your choice will appear in relation to others. Each house style will probably have a different price tag, but houses of the same style can also vary in price depending on their site location or plot size; some, for example, may have a larger garden or a more pleasant outlook.

> **MONEY-SAVING TIP**
> Submit your offer to the building company direct, as well as the on-site sales staff. The sales staff will want to get the best price, whereas the company may be willing to take an offer in order to shift stock.

When visiting a new site, even if the building work is still in progress, you need to view the site as a whole and ask yourself some basic, but important, questions.

- Will the site be more cramped on completion than the plan indicates?
- Is there sufficient parking, not only for your vehicles but for visitors and other home owners?
- Are there any communal garden areas, and if so, who looks after them?
- Does the arrangement of the site appeal to you?
- How long will it be before all construction work is completed? You do not want to be living in the middle of a building site indefinitely.

- Are other sites planned in the immediate vicinity?

On this final point, be aware that small developments have a habit of growing into large estates. Make sure that what you are viewing is not just Phase 1, with other phases planned for construction around it.

Take a look at where your chosen house is situated on the site. The position of the property within an estate is vitally important, especially when it comes to selling it at some time in the future. When the appeal of its newness is gone, it will be just one of many. For example, if it is at the head of the estate, all access traffic will pass your door, or the shape of the back garden may mean that a lot of other gardens back on to yours, reducing privacy.

MONEY-SAVING TIP

If your chosen property is in a good position, but more expensive as a result, you may be able to negotiate the price in line with other properties of the same style if your buying position is good.

If the site already has residents, then clearly the best people to speak to about buying a property there are those who already have, so knock on a few doors and don't be shy to ask some searching questions. If you know about these things in advance, you will be able to make sure you get exactly what you are paying for. You also get the opportunity to see what the neighbours are like.

- Ask about the build quality – was the finish as good as the show home?
- If any defects appeared after completion, were they remedied quickly?
- Was the building completed on schedule?

- Were the fittings, such as bathroom and kitchen, to a good standard?
- What about the garden areas – were they turfed and/or paved as expected?

Finally, try to find out about the land being built on. Does it have an industrial past or a history of flooding? Perhaps the area has previously been mined? New homes have been, and will continue to be, built on flood plains, to the amazement of local people who know the area and have seen it regularly under water. One resource that is extremely useful, and simple to use, is the flood-risk map created by the Environment Agency, which shows whether an area has a low, moderate or high risk of flooding. This is updated quarterly so the information is always current.

Your solicitor should carry out an Environmental Search, which will highlight areas of possible concern, but if you have specific concerns then do ask him to carry out more specific searches.

SMALL OR INDIVIDUAL DEVELOPMENTS

Not all new homes are built on large sites. Some are built singularly by the owner of a piece of land, or else are conversions; perhaps of a barn or by splitting one house into several flats. Whilst large building companies have their reputation to commend them (or not, as the case may be), it is difficult to tell with small developments or conversions if the builder or developer is of good repute. Bear in mind also that, while a large company will usually rectify any future problems as a matter of company procedure, an individual builder may prove more difficult to tie down to any 'after-sales service'.

SHOW HOMES - STAYING REALISTIC

Most builders prepare a show home to entice potential buyers. At first glance these show homes seem simply to demonstrate how the building functions as a normal home, with carefully placed items giving a 'lived-in' look, as though the owners have just stepped out. However, everything is a little too carefully arranged to be a true depiction of what the place will look like when someone really does move in, and some very clever tricks are used to make the space as attractive as possible.

It is easy to be bowled over by a show home, but it pays to remember that the property you move into will bear little resemblance to what you see there. The interior designer who decorated the show home with such care and attention to detail won't be decorating your new home. This job will be passed on to a member of the construction team who will do little more than slap on a quick coat of paint.

Also, as with any property, you're not buying the furniture, so try not to take too much notice of it. Furniture used in show homes has been designed to fit by an expert, to make each room look its very best, and none of the little touches like coordinating soft furnishings and clever lighting will be included in the price. Be focused and savvy and look out for these common tricks of the trade.

- Lights left on, even in daylight, to make rooms seem light and airy.
- Smaller than average furniture used to make rooms appear larger. Often large items of furniture are left out completely, such as wardrobes, because they take up too much space.
- The salesman will usually invite you to enter each room first, so that he stays out of the line of vision and does not crowd the limited space.
- Interior doors propped open (or not even hung) because an object as large as a door takes up valuable space.
- Personal effects are limited to the essentials. You, on the other hand, will have all the paraphernalia that comes with everyday life.
- Furniture and decoration is usually in pale colours to make rooms look larger.

- Window sizes are exaggerated with carefully arranged curtains and blinds.

One of the main drawbacks of a new house is that the rooms are often small, hence why most of the ploys used above are aimed at increasing the illusion of space. It may be an obvious warning to give, but do make sure your furniture will fit, and that you can position it how you like it instead of the only way it will fit into the rooms. Serious design defects are rare, but it is not uncommon to view a show home and not realize, for example, that the smallest bedroom has room for a single bed but nothing else.

THE BUYING PROCESS

After you have viewed the show home, you will be given lots of promotional leaflets to take away with you, giving information on the type of heating installed, what fixtures and fittings are included, construction details, local amenities and the all-important price list. In most cases the price is negotiable in the same way as a 'second-hand' property, especially if you are in a good buying position and have either exchanged contracts on the sale of your current property or have nothing to sell. The only difference is that negotiations may be direct with the seller, and not through an estate agent, unless of course an agency is marketing the site.

> **MONEY-SAVING TIP**
> Builders may be open to negotiation at the beginning of a building phase. A good advertisement for the site is the number of houses sold, so they are keen to sell some quickly to encourage other buyers. Towards the end of the project can also be a good time to negotiate the price, as the builders are keen to clear the last few unsold properties to complete the project.

If you have not yet sold your current property the builder may be willing to reserve the home of your choice until you can find a buyer yourself and are in a position to go ahead with the purchase. You will usually be expected to pay a reservation fee to show your commitment, which is fair enough, but do get written confirmation that the builder will return the reservation fee if he withdraws from the sale, and that the amount of the reservation fee will be deducted from the purchase price when the sale completes.

A final point to bear in mind when buying a new property is that it takes a lot of time and money to turn an empty shell into a home. All the little things generally included as standard in a second-hand home will need to be bought for a new home. This includes such things as curtain rails, towel rails, bathroom cabinets, light fittings, floor coverings, coat hooks and more, and all these little extras can add up to a hefty sum.

BUYING OFF PLAN

If you are buying completely 'off plan', in other words the construction of the site has yet to start or has barely begun, you can expect to pay up to 20 per cent less than the market value. In theory, the value of the property could increase in the time it takes for construction to be completed, so in effect 'your' property is gaining value before you have even paid for it.

All the points about buying a new-build home apply to buying off plan, and you could make a wise investment this way. BUT, and it is an intentionally big but, there are potential downfalls that you should bear in mind.

- The value of the property could go down if the property market falls.
- The date for completion will be very flexible.
- The finished property might not be quite what you expected.

- You could be living with noise and disruption while the site is under construction.

WARRANTIES

The NHBC is a UK organization that regulates its members in the house-building industry. NHBC members have to demonstrate their ability to build to a qualifying standard, and new homes which carry the NHBC Buildmark 10-year warranty have been subjected to visits by inspectors to make sure the buildings comply with construction criteria. This is important because someone who buys a new home only sees it after it has been built, when construction practices that could cause problems in the fabric of the building are no longer visible. Under the Buildmark warranty, buyers are insured against faults that occur as a result of non-compliance with Building Regulations.

The NHBC Buildmark warranty aims to protect buyers in three ways. Firstly, if you purchase a property still under construction, the NHBC protects against financial loss due to incomplete construction if the builder declares himself bankrupt. Secondly, during the first two years of ownership, the NHBC ensures that builders honour their obligation to rectify faults that are in breach of their standards. Lastly, from the third to tenth year of ownership, the NHBC itself bears the cost of remedial work to correct major problems caused by structural defects.

MONEY-SAVING TIP

If you construct an extension to a new-build home, or perhaps a conservatory, this addition will not be covered by the NHBC policy. If the original property is damaged in the course of construction, this will not be covered either. This could result in a very expensive mistake, so be sure to get professional advice, obtain all necessary approvals and employ competent contractors.

There is no charge to you for the Buildmark warranty, since the builder pays the one-off premium. However, if you make a claim after the second year of ownership, a fee will be charged before the claim can be processed. If your claim is accepted, this fee is refunded. If you make a claim before the second year, which goes to arbitration and the ruling falls against you, you must bear the costs of arbitration. As with any form of insurance, the policy should be read carefully so that you know about any exclusions and restrictions.

There can be no doubt that the NHBC warranty is worth having, not least because inspections during the course of construction should prevent defects occurring in the first place. However, the warranty should not be relied upon to give 10 years of free repairs: wear and tear is not covered.

The building still needs to be insured – the NHBC is not a buildings insurance policy and will certainly not pay out for accidental damage, such as a tree falling through the roof or lightning causing the place to burn to the ground.

Some builders offer a Zurich Building Guarantee, which is similar to the NHBC Buildmark.

'RUNNING IN' A NEW HOME

Problems with the fabric of a new building are no more likely than with that of a second-hand property, but a new house does need a period of running in, mainly to safeguard against the number one enemy of any building: water.

During construction, the building will have absorbed water – lots of it. Most of the materials, such as wood, brick and plaster, are porous, so the building starts off damp and needs to dry out gently. As this drying out occurs, the wood and plaster often shrink and begin to show tiny cracks. At the same time, moisture is released into the air and can cause condensation.

These problems are unavoidable, but can be kept to a minimum by heating the property gently and evenly, and helping air to circulate by leaving windows and internal doors open as much as possible. Most of the condensation caused by the damp building materials will ease once the property is occupied. Condensation on windows should be wiped away as soon as it appears, to avoid permanent damage to the frame.

Once you have moved into your new home, you should draw up a 'snag list' of any problems you find, such as ill-fitting doors or leaking taps, and present this list to the builder for him to rectify the faults. On a large site this is usually done quickly because there are carpenters, plumbers and other tradespeople working on the site all the time.

Resist the temptation to redecorate your new home until it has properly dried out. This could take around six months, but ask the builder's advice. If you paint or paper over still-damp walls, you will end up with a poor finish and will only find yourself doing it again.

IN SUMMARY

- Make sure the builder is on the NHBC register (or similar).
- Don't get carried away by the lure of pristine show homes.
- Check the history of the site for possible flooding or other environmental issues.
- Make sure you know what to expect from the standard of finish. Will the garden be turfed? Will the loft be boarded? Will the bathroom be tiled?
- Get written confirmation of any extras, such as your choice of kitchen units, bathroom suite or floor coverings.
- If possible, tie the builder down to a specific completion date.
- Make sure a reservation deposit is returnable if the builder withdraws from the sale.
- Make sure you know what restrictions there are. For example, you may not be allowed to fence the front garden area.

Chapter 7
BUYING AT AUCTION

IS AN AUCTION RIGHT FOR YOU?

The number of properties bought and sold at auction accounts for only a small percentage of general property transactions, mainly because the auction system is an unknown quantity for the majority of us. For most people, making an offer direct to the seller (known as the 'private treaty' system) seems far easier and less daunting than making a bid at auction.

However, buying at auction could save you thousands. Most property that comes to auction is sold that way for speed and certainty of sale, so banks and housing associations commonly use this method to dispose of property quickly, and that often means cheaply. The financial drawback, though, is that if your bid fails, any outlay you will have made in legal fees or surveys will be lost. But there are bargains to be had, so it's worth considering this type of buying.

The obvious thing to understand is that once a bid is accepted and the hammer falls, the commitment to buy is binding. Unlike the private treaty system, which allows you time to back out of the purchase if you change your mind or perhaps cannot raise the finance, if you buy at auction you must have your finances in place before the auction and there is no going back.

Even if a successful bidder leaves the auction without signing the contract of sale, the auctioneer can sign the contract on his behalf and the sale is still binding.

Some people reject buying at auction out of hand because they do not know how the process works, and worry that bidding might happen so quickly that the property they want to buy is sold before they have a chance to bid. Auctions do tend to be fairly crowded, and it's a nerve-racking experience, but as long as you are prepared, it's actually a much simpler way of buying a property – not least because the seller cannot pull out at the last minute. If you make the winning bid, the property is yours.

Perhaps the biggest misconception about buying at auction is that you need to be a cash buyer. In fact, in many cases it is perfectly possible to obtain a mortgage in the usual way. It is essential to plan ahead to arrange funding in advance (as well as some of the initial conveyancing work and a survey or valuation), but it is not impossible. Unfortunately, as mentioned above, if your bid is unsuccessful, any costs incurred in putting mortgage funding in place before the auction will be wasted.

WHAT TYPE OF PROPERTY IS SOLD AT AUCTION?

Buyers often imagine that the only type of property on offer at an auction will be mortgage repossessions or properties in unpopular areas and in poor condition, and it's true to say that these do account for a reasonable percentage of auctioned properties – but not all. Because many people who buy at auction nowadays are owner-occupiers, and not just builders or property speculators, there is a wider variety of property sold this way.

Almost any property can be sold at auction, but some traditionally sell more successfully than others, particularly those worth less than £200,000 and in need of renovation or improvement.

Properties like these generally attract a good attendance of potential buyers, and competition pushes the price up. All it takes for an auction to be successful, and for the price to increase, is for two or more buyers to want the same thing.

Whilst it is possible to pick up a good buy at auction, it's a mistake to assume that all auction property is a bargain. You must do your homework on any property you are interested in, because sometimes an auction is so successful that the property sells for more than the market value.

Properties in need of renovation attract a lot of interested buyers, especially if the guide price (see below) is temptingly low, because this type of property can seem like a good buy compared to similar properties in good condition. A word of warning, though – buying such a property can be a false economy, because more often than not the renovation work will be far more expensive than you think. You may see a basically sound building, which simply needs tidying up – a new kitchen and bathroom, replacement windows, new central heating and general decorating. No problem. A few thousand pounds should be enough, and most of the work can be done by a DIY enthusiast without the expense of employing professionals.

However, it is very hard work, especially if you plan to do most of the labour yourself, and if you need to employ a team of builders and craftsmen, the expense of this, plus the initial purchase price, can outweigh the value of the finished property. It's imperative therefore to know before the auction exactly how much the improvements will cost before deciding how much it is worth bidding.

Bear in mind also that living in a property while improvements are being carried out can be difficult. The persistent dust and upheaval quickly becomes trying, and the work usually goes on for much longer than expected. Of course it is all worth it to get the home of your dreams, but you could find after all your hard work that you could have bought, for what you have spent or less, a similar property that someone else has slaved over.

If you buy a property in need of serious renovation, through an auction or otherwise, you will only be able to obtain funding to buy the property in its current state – its estimated value before the renovation. You may need to arrange additional funding, or a staged mortgage (see page 51), to fund the renovation work.

This is also the case when buying land to build on. A mortgage can be secured on the land itself, but not on the new building until it is built. Some lenders will arrange staged loans, which enable you to draw down funds as the building is constructed, and hence it gains value of its own.

PRICING

The price paid for an auction property will only be determined on the day, so it's impossible to know in advance how much this will be. Much will depend on how well the event has been promoted, and consequently the number of bidders. When an auction property is advertised, the agents will give an idea of what they think the property is worth, but this is really only an estimate.

Guide price
The guide price is the advertised price, and is usually lower than the seller expects to achieve. The figure is pitched to attract as much

interest as possible, so that on the day of the auction there are plenty of eager bidders in competition with each other. It is unrealistic to assume you will secure a property for a bid of the guide price; it is not even necessarily an indication of the reserve price (see below).

Reserve price

This is the lowest price the seller is willing to sell for, and the auctioneer will not accept a final bid that is lower than this amount. The existence of a reserve price will be mentioned in the auctioneer's Conditions of Sale, although the actual figure remains confidential. If no one bids above the reserve price, the property will remain unsold. The auctioneer may start the bidding below the reserve price, since he wants to encourage plenty of lively bidding to start proceedings.

PREPARING FOR AN AUCTION

Many estate agencies now handle actions, and it's easy to find those who do from the Internet. Armed with this information, you can register with the relevant agents and auctioneers so that in due course you will receive details of properties to be auctioned. If any of them are of interest, arrange for an appointment to view in the usual way.

The number of properties offered at any one auction varies from one event to another. Most auction houses (or agencies) produce a catalogue of upcoming events, showing the properties that will be sold and giving information on the process.

Once you find a property worth bidding on, you will need to start preparing in advance of the auction date. Make sure that all the necessary administrative preparations listed below are in place prior to an auction, but even more importantly, you must prepare yourself. Before attending the auction, you should know exactly what the property is worth and should not be tempted to bid above this figure. This maximum may not necessarily be the most you can afford, but it is as much as the property is worth. If you know yourself well enough to suspect that having a sensible maximum in mind might not be enough to halt the temptation to bid higher, you could ask your solicitor to attend the auction and bid on your behalf, up to an agreed limit.

FUNDING

If you need a mortgage, this must be arranged in advance, so that funding is in place on the day of the auction, although obviously you will not know exactly what you will ultimately pay for the property until your bid is successful.

Your lenders may not be concerned with the amount you actually pay for the property, but they will specify in the mortgage offer the maximum they are prepared to lend, and the percentage of loan to value.

For example, if you intend to purchase for £100,000 (and the lender is happy with this as a valuation) and have agreed a 75 per cent mortgage, your mortgage amount will be £75,000 and your deposit £25,000.

However, if you pay more on the day, say £120,000, you *may* be able to increase your mortgage to 75 per cent of that amount (£90,000) but you will have to be prepared to increase your deposit to £45,000 if you can't.

If you pay less for the property, say £90,000, the amount of your mortgage will reduce (although the percentage will still be 75 per cent), as will your deposit. In this case, the mortgage offer will need to be amended as soon as possible.

SURVEY

Before issuing a mortgage offer, the lender will want a valuation report carried out to ascertain the property's value and condition. The lender will probably arrange this in the usual way. A survey is just as necessary for an auction purchase as it is for a conventional purchase. If the property is in a state of disrepair, the lenders may insist on a detailed report, and may impose a retention. For instance, they may withhold part of the loan until the repairs are completed.

If the property needs renovating, it would be a good idea to get quotes for the work before the auction, so that you can see exactly what your costs will be.

CONVEYANCING

Certain aspects of the conveyancing need to be carried out in advance of the auction to ensure that the purchase goes smoothly and to protect you, but the paperwork involved is much the same as for a normal purchase.

Your solicitor will obtain the usual information about the property and report to you in the same way as any other conveyance, although some of the information he would normally obtain will be supplied to all potential purchasers by the auctioneers in the form of an Auction Pack, including searches. However, if the property is being sold by a bank as a repossession, or by an attorney for a deceased estate or similar, the seller will have little knowledge of the property and it will be up to you and your solicitor to check anything important.

The contract must be ready for signature on the day of the auction. In order for you to be in a position to sign the contract, your solicitor will approve it, and the Transfer document, before the auction.

The exchange of contracts happens on the day, and legally binds you to complete the purchase. Completion usually takes place 14–28 days after exchange of contracts, or earlier if both parties agree.

DEPOSIT

A deposit, usually 10 per cent of the purchase price, is paid by the buyer on the day of the auction, either to the auctioneer direct by way of a cheque or between the solicitors acting for both parties. You must therefore have sufficient funds readily available to pay this on the day of the auction.

INSURANCE

If your bid is successful, you must put buildings insurance in place immediately. This is because you now have a 10 per cent interest in the property and are committed to buy it even if it burns down between the auction and the date of completion. Your lender, if you have one, will also insist on this. Before the auction, speak to your insurers so that on the day you only need to give them a quick call to confirm that cover needs to be in force immediately.

MONEY-SAVING TIP

Familiarise yourself with the system, by going along to one or two auctions as an observer, before attending an auction with the intention of bidding.

ATTENDING AN AUCTION

A few days before the auction date you should confirm with your solicitor that all the necessary paperwork is in place. That is to say, the searches are in order, all other information has been received and is satisfactory, and the contract approved. You will by this time have arranged mortgage funding if necessary, and the survey or valuation will have been carried out. Your deposit will be immediately available, and all that remains is to secure the purchase on the day.

Auctions are not always held in auction rooms. Sometimes a village hall or local hotel is used, or indeed the property itself, so make sure you know where the venue is.

There is no need to arrive at the auction venue particularly early, but do allow sufficient travelling time to avoid arriving late or having to hurry. You will need to register on arrival, so allow time for this, and remember to take along the required form of ID. There could be several properties being auctioned, and this will give you a chance to watch other sales before the auctioneer starts the bidding on the one you are interested in.

If the bidding is slow to start, the auctioneer can make bids himself up to the reserve price. This is common practice, but not usually noticeable to the untrained eye, so you might assume quite wrongly that other people are making bids. The auctioneer is not acting inappropriately – the seller, via the auctioneer, commonly holds the right to bid to the reserve price.

The way to make a bid is simply to attract the auctioneer's attention by, for example, raising your hand. Once the auctioneer sees that you are bidding, he will look towards you periodically to see if you wish to increase your bid.

The auctioneer cannot make you bid against yourself. In other words, if you make a bid above the reserve price and nobody answers the auctioneer's next price call, he cannot look to you to better your last bid, so the property becomes yours. If the price keeps rising, you know someone else is in competition with you, or bidding has not yet reached the reserve price.

If your bid is successful, you will be expected to pay the deposit straight away. Details of your solicitor are requested, although often in practice your solicitor and the solicitor acting for the seller will have liaised already.

BIDDING – KEEPING YOUR COOL

At the end of the day, you must accept that you will lose out one way or another if someone else is interested in the same property as you and is willing to bid higher. Either you will fail to secure the property, or you will pay more than it is worth.

The latter is of course to be avoided, but you can see how easily it can happen. You start bidding tentatively, then gain confidence as other buyers drop out. The bidding edges towards your maximum, but now it's a two-horse race. The remaining competitor looks comfortable, so you wonder if he could be an investor. If so, reason suggests he has to make a profit, so you know he will not pay over the odds.

You make your maximum bid confidently, but your competitor raises his hand again. Perhaps he knows something you don't. The auctioneer looks to you to raise the stakes with another bid. You make one more. The property, previously desirable, is suddenly absolutely essential to you. The competition makes another bid, taking the price past your maximum, but still affordable, so you raise your hand again. A pause, then the auctioneer takes another bid from the opposition. You fume inwardly, but bid again, confident of success because you know the property isn't worth any more.

One more bid should do it. The competitor raises the stakes once more. Well, two can play at that game. SUCCESS. The competitor shakes his head and you are the proud owner. But at what cost?

MONEY-SAVING TIP

Never attend an auction with the intention of 'going with the flow'. Know your limit and stick to it.

If a property fails to meet its reserve price (see page 93), this doesn't necessarily mean it will be withdrawn from sale, and you could approach the auctioneer to see if he is able to do a deal with you, as agent for the seller. This can be a good way to pick up a bargain, because the seller has obviously been overly ambitious about the price and may be prepared to take a reduction to get the property sold on the day.

Similarly, a property may be sold prior to auction if a deal can be made, so it's worth asking the agents about this (see page 100).

COSTS

The costs involved in purchasing at auction are much the same as purchasing on the open market, and since your solicitor will need to carry out much of the conveyancing prior to the auction, you will be asked for payment on account to cover the cost of disbursements incurred before the auction. If you are not successful at the auction, you will still incur some costs:

• Solicitor fees
• Arrangement fee (charged by lender)
• Valuation or survey

If you buy at auction with your own funds, you can avoid losing money on unsuccessful bids by not having a survey, but only if you are confident and competent enough to buy without one. Similarly, cash buyers might only employ a solicitor if their bid is successful, but they run the risk of acquiring a property with a dubious title or problematic searches if these are not checked beforehand.

COMPLETION

Since much of the conveyance work is done in advance of the auction, and there is no chain involved, completion on a property bought at auction can be achieved quickly. Usually this takes place around 14–28 days after the auction, but in theory it could be as soon as the following day if both buyer and seller agree, and if the solicitors have completed the paperwork.

The conveyance procedure post exchange of contracts is much the same as for private treaty purchases. If the property being bought has a mortgage secured on it, the seller's solicitor arranges for this to be redeemed, and if you are using a mortgage the funds will be registered in the usual way.

The date for completion is included in the contract, so since your solicitor will already have seen the contract, you will know this date before the auction. Completion takes place in the usual way, when solicitors acting for both parties oversee the transfer of documents and delivery of purchase funds. The key is then made available so that you can take possession.

OFFERS PRIOR TO AUCTION

If you wish, you can sometimes approach the selling agents or auctioneers and make an offer for a property before it goes to auction. If your offer is accepted, the property is then withdrawn from the auction, but only if the contract of sale is signed before the date of the intended auction. If not, the seller may allow the auction to continue, because his concern is that you could back out of the purchase, leaving him high and dry. If the seller refuses your offer and the auction goes ahead but the property fails to reach its reserve price, the seller might then reconsider your offer. Since it is then obvious that the auction failed, this could put you in a strong negotiating position.

TELEPHONE AUCTIONS

Sometimes the selling agent may instigate an unofficial telephone auction. If, for example, the agents receive an offer prior to auction from Mr First, they may then telephone Mrs Second, who has also shown an interest in the property. The agent explains that the seller is considering an offer prior to auction (although he should not disclose the offer amount), and asks if Mrs Second would also like to make an offer. Mrs Second might refuse, or she might make an offer, which she hopes is higher than Mr First's.

If it is, the agent then goes back to Mr First with the bad news that a higher offer has been received, in response to which Mr First might increase his own offer. If so, the agent returns to Mrs Second to see if she will better her offer, and so on, until both potential buyers have their cards on the table and the highest offer is reached. Understandably, this system is not popular with buyers, and the property may still go to auction if the final offer is not high enough.

BEST OFFERS

If an agent is marketing a property for auction but a disappointing level of interest makes him doubt it will reach its reserve, he may use another method to prompt a sale prior to the auction, by inviting written offers to be received by a particular date. Because potential buyers do not know what other potential buyers will offer, or even if there are any, the agents hope that the interested buyers will submit their very best offers or risk losing out to a higher bidder. When the offers are received, the seller has the option of accepting the best one or taking his chances at auction, as originally planned.

A good offer will only be accepted if the buyer is able to meet a deadline to sign the contract of sale. If he is not able to meet this deadline, the property will usually still go to auction, or alternatively the next best offer may be accepted in the same way if there is sufficient time. From the seller's point of view, he may well attract more offers this way than he could expect to receive from buyers who might be unable or unwilling to bid at auction.

Potential buyers often find this arrangement preferable to bidding at auction because they do not have any expenses if their bid is not accepted. However, this type of bid is not binding, and the buyer or seller can withdraw at any time before contracts are exchanged.

Both of the above systems force buyers to bid in the dark, in that they do not know the amount of other offers and they only have the agent's word for it that there are any. Agents usually reserve the right to reject offers, even the best ones, if they consider they are not good enough and a better price might be gained at auction.

ADVANTAGES AND DISADVANTAGES
OF BUYING AT AUCTION

The main advantage of auctions to both buyer and seller is that they can save time and circumvent a lot of uncertainty. Because the purchase is secured on the day, there is no chain involved and the period between the auction and completion is usually a month or less. The seller has the advantage of knowing that the property will almost certainly be sold on the day, assuming the reserve price is met.

The disadvantages manly affect potential buyers. You can go to a lot of trouble to prepare for an auction and then be out-bid by the competition, losing the property and incurring costs. Also, there is no 'cooling off' period between making an offer and exchange of contracts, which there is in the private treaty system, during which you could back out of the purchase if you had a change of heart.

And lastly, if you are not careful, you could end up paying more for a property than its market value. Aside from the temptation to out-bid the competition, this can also happen because property sold at auction is sometimes unique, so without knowledge of comparable properties it is difficult to estimate a true value.

IN SUMMARY

- Research the market – know what the property is worth before you bid on it.
- Attend a few auctions as an observer to gain confidence and understanding of the system.
- Visit the property as you would normally.
- Have the property surveyed and get estimates for repairs if necessary.
- Have a very clear maximum bid in mind before you attend the auction, and stick to it.
- Consider making an offer prior to auction.

Chapter 8
CONVEYANCING

"How sweet – the solicitor has given us a welcome mat."

CORDIAL FELICITATIONS ON EGRESS TO YOUR NEWLY-ACQUIRED DOMICILE

DEALING WITH THE LEGAL WORK

Buying a property – the process of transferring ownership from one person to another – involves unavoidable paperwork. Lots of it. Documents have to be drawn up for signature by both buyer and seller, information must be obtained and conditions agreed. It can be a lengthy process, not because it is particularly complex, but because it relies on a lot of people to supply information.

The seller needs to supply documents and information relating to the property, the buyer has to supply information to secure his funding, the lender needs information on the property, and so it goes on. The people who orchestrate and collect this veritable mountain of paperwork, who hopefully have their finger on the pulse of proceedings, are the conveyancers or solicitors acting for buyer and seller.

The same solicitor cannot act for both buyer and seller, as this could lead to a conflict of interest. However, two solicitors from the same firm can act for both parties – one for the buyer and one for the seller, as long as both parties are existing clients of the firm.

> **MONEY-SAVING TIP**
>
> Solicitors in major cities have high overheads, so charge high fees. Consider using a solicitor in a less-expensive area – your solicitor does not have to be local.

CHOOSING A SOLICITOR

Solicitors do not have a monopoly on conveyancing, and you could alternatively use a licensed conveyancer. He or she will not be a qualified solicitor but can act in the legal transfer of property, which in most cases is all you need. For purposes of simplicity, the term 'solicitor' has been used to refer to any legal representative.

If you already employ a solicitor for other matters, or have used a particular firm in the past, you may want to instruct them to handle the conveyance, but do get quotes from other firms too, as fees can vary enormously.

> **MONEY-SAVING TIP**
>
> Many firms of solicitors employ licensed conveyancers or legal executives. They should do just as good a job as a solicitor, but their fees will often be lower.

If you need a solicitor to deal with other matters at the same time as the conveyance, for example if you are moving home because of a divorce, it may be useful to have one solicitor or firm dealing with both matters, cutting down on correspondence delays and time generally.

If you are buying and selling simultaneously you can use one solicitor for both transactions, and from an administrative point of view this is preferable. It doesn't matter if you are buying and selling in different parts of the country, since your solicitor does not need to be local to either property. However, it does help if your solicitor has knowledge of the area you are buying into, especially if it is not known to you, since he may know about general plans for the region that are not common knowledge, and will also be aware of what searches are standard for that area.

FEES – KEEPING THEM LOW

Get quotes from several different firms to get an idea of average fees. Charges are usually based on the value of the property, so solicitors will want to know the purchase price of the property you are buying before they give you a quote.

Legal charges for buying a leasehold property are often higher than for a freehold property, because there is extra work involved in approving the lease and ensuring service charges and any other financial commitments are paid up to date.

> **MONEY-SAVING TIP**
> For a leasehold purchase, ensure your solicitor gives a fixed-fee quote that cannot be increased if the process takes longer than anticipated, which is quite likely.

You will also need to consider other costs, such as search fees, Stamp Duty Land Tax and Land Registry charges, so ask your solicitor for a breakdown of *all* costs when he gives you his quote.

If your transaction takes considerably longer than anticipated, the end fee may be higher than the quote, unless you have a fixed fee arrangement. Solicitors use time-recording systems to record exactly how much time has been spent on your transaction: the number of telephone calls in and out, how many letters have been written and other tasks within the process. If this adds up to substantially more than the original quote, the final charge will be higher. Solicitors are obliged to keep you informed if costs are likely to exceed their quote.

Once you have agreed a fee with your solicitor, send an email or letter clarifying details of the property (address, purchase price, details of the selling agents), your own details and the agreed fee. If he hasn't already done so, ask your solicitor to clarify any other costs you can expect to incur, which will help you to budget. You should then receive an official engagement letter setting out the firm's terms of business, their obligations to you, their fees and other costs. On a property costing £200,000, the figures would look something like this:

Legal fees	500.00
VAT @ 20%	100.00
Search fees – Local Authority,	
Water & Drainage (estimated)	300.00
Land Registry fees	140.00
Stamp Duty Land Tax @ 1%	2,000.00
Telegraphic transfer fee (incl VAT)	42.00
Bankruptcy search fee	2.00
Land Registry search fee	3.00
Total	£3,227.00

You will probably be asked to pay your solicitor some money 'on account' so that searches can be ordered. Your solicitor will only request these searches when he has the money from you to pay for them, so don't delay in getting this to him. If there is any money left over from this up-front payment, it will be accounted for in the final statement – in other words, it will come off the bill.

MONEY-SAVING TIP
Watch out for extra charges and disbursements, especially with 'cut-price' conveyancers. The legal fees may look low at first glance, but when you factor in these extras, they may not be so competitive.

WORKING TOGETHER

The longer your purchase takes to complete, the higher your legal fees are likely to be (unless you have a fixed-fee arrangement). The best way to avoid rising costs, and to get the best out of your solicitor, is to work with him.

If he asks you to obtain a particular piece of information, or to sign something in the presence of a witness, do it promptly and do it correctly. If your solicitor has to re-send documents to you, or struggles to contact you, it wastes his valuable time and causes unnecessary delays.

In most cases, the purchase of a property follows a simple process. The seller provides various items of information to the buyer (or more particularly, his solicitor), and the solicitor acting for the buyer checks that all the documentation is in order and reports his findings to the buyer. This process is not usually complicated, but it is time consuming.

Here are some ways you can speed up the process by being proactive:

- Mortgage funding can take time to arrange. If you need to move quickly, explain the situation to your lender (or mortgage broker) and ask them to fast track your application. Once your application has been agreed in principle, you will need to chase the lender to obtain your official Mortgage Offer (see page 52). As soon as you receive this, make sure your solicitor has received his copy. You may need to formally accept the offer, so don't delay in doing this.

- If you have any specific queries about the property, mention these to your solicitor straight away. He can include them with his standard enquiries, rather than having to deal with them as a separate issue.

- Your solicitor may ask you for funds on account (commonly around £300) to pay for search fees. Get this to him as soon as you can, as he will not put the searches in hand until he has it.

- Keep in touch with the selling agents. Just because the seller is paying their fee, they still have a job to do for you. If things slow down, ask them to chase the seller's solicitors. Solicitors will sometimes tell the agents more than they tell the other party's solicitors.

- Speak regularly to your solicitor or their secretary to ensure your file remains a priority and is not lingering at the bottom of the pile.

When you consider that conveyancing mainly involves obtaining and checking information and documentation, you can see how thinking ahead and keeping up the pace can significantly speed up the process.

> **MONEY-SAVING TIP**
> Find out the name of your solicitor's secretary. Legal secretaries are very knowledgeable but don't charge for their time, so they may be able to answer some of your queries free of charge.

The selling agents' details will give your solicitor some valuable information, so you should certainly make sure he has a copy of these. For example, the details may mention that 'access is obtained down a private road'. You may not see this as a problem, and it might not be one, but your solicitor needs to clarify whether or not the road is 'private' as a description of its seclusion, or whether it is private property. If it's the latter, clarification will be needed on rights over the road, and who is responsible for repair and maintenance.

The agents' details will not, however, tell your solicitor everything, and since he is unlikely to visit the property on your behalf, it is helpful to mention your own observations. If, for example, it seems likely that two rooms have been knocked into one, mention this to your solicitor, as he will want to obtain documents confirming that the structural work was carried out according to the relevant building regulations.

Similarly, mention to your solicitor any additions to the original building so that he can check these out. If there is a new garage or extension, for example, the seller will need to supply documented evidence that the work was approved by the local authority. If building work does not have the necessary planning permission, the local authority is empowered (for a limited period) to demand its removal, although in such cases an indemnity insurance policy may be taken out to protect you.

If there is anything about the property you are unsure of, or would like clarification on, don't be shy to ask your solicitor about it. That's what you are paying him for.

Finally, clarify the name of the particular solicitor who will be handling your file. If you need to speak to him, ask for him personally. Do not accept being dealt with by whoever answers the call; they will not be fully aware of your case or any particular concerns you may have. It is worth clarifying whether your particular solicitor works full time, or you may find that he is difficult to contact, and on the days he is out of the office your file might be left gathering dust.

> **MONEY-SAVING TIP**
>
> You may wish to see the result of a survey before going ahead with a purchase. If this is the case, ask your solicitor not to put in hand searches or read through the contract documentation until you are happy to proceed. This could save you a lot of money in legal charges if the survey is unsatisfactory and you decide to pull out of the purchase.

THE LEGAL PROCESS

The mountain of paper used in each property purchase probably costs the life of a small tree, and you can expect to receive from your solicitor a stream of documents that need signature, approval or both. The process mostly follows a set pattern of steps.

STEP 1 – GATHERING INFORMATION

The first thing your solicitor needs to do, is find out everything he can about the property itself and its title (who owns it). He will do this by requesting information from the seller's solicitors and through his own investigations.

Fittings and contents

At the outset of a purchase, you need to clarify exactly what, apart from the bricks and mortar, is included in the purchase price. The seller may be leaving carpets and curtains, or he may strip the place down to the boards. Either is acceptable, so long as there is agreement between you and the seller about what will be left in the property as part of the purchase.

You will probably have discussed this with the seller when you viewed the property, but for clarification your solicitor will obtain a completed Fittings and Contents Form from the seller, showing what is included, excluded or not at the property, and what items can be purchased for an additional fee. You will receive a copy of this and should look through it carefully to make sure the seller has not gone back on what was agreed.

If anything is wrongly shown as excluded from the sale, you should advise your solicitor accordingly. The seller may well adopt a take-it-or-leave-it attitude, but it might be possible to negotiate a reduction in the purchase price if the cost of the item under discussion is worth haggling over.

Some fixtures and fittings are automatically included in the purchase price, like fitted cupboards, plumbing and electrical fittings, and the plants in the garden (excluding those in containers), but other items like freestanding appliances (a fridge or washing machine that is not built in), are often removed by the seller as his personal possessions.

Property Information Form and Leasehold Information Form

Again, a standard form is used, asking general questions about the property for the seller to answer.

- Boundaries.
- Past or ongoing disputes with neighbours.
- Alterations made to the property.
- Details of maintenance or service checks.
- Details of the connected services.
- Parking arrangements.
- Building works completed, such as extensions.
- Guarantees for work done.

The seller is required to give truthful replies to the questions. If he does not know the answer, he must say so. The form may therefore be littered with vague answers like 'don't know' or 'not to my knowledge'. If anything needs clarification, you will need to ask your solicitor to make his own enquiries.

Energy Performance Certificate

All sellers are obligated to obtain an Energy Performance Certificate for the property they are selling. This shows the overall energy efficiency of the home, and the more energy efficient the home is, the lower the fuel bills are likely to be. It also shows the environmental impact of the property in terms of emissions.

Local authority search

Your solicitor will send a search application to the local authority. The information supplied discloses such things as whether the property is a listed building and whether there are road schemes planned in the immediate vicinity, but not everything will be marked against the property. If you have any particular concerns it is imperative that you discuss them with your solicitor, who can then make further enquiries as necessary.

The search will also disclose whether the property has been granted planning permission for any building work, and whether such work has building-regulation approval. The rules are complex, so any building work will need clarification. Your solicitor will obtain a copy of any planning permissions. If the seller is unable to provide evidence of consents, your solicitor may suggest taking out indemnity insurance to protect you in the event that consent is later found to have been declined. The cost of such a policy will usually be borne by the seller.

It is important to understand that the searches do not give information on land or property outside the boundaries of the property you are buying, so if you need information on a particular issue relating to adjoining or nearby land or property you will either have to carry out your own investigations or request a specialist search.

For example, a local search will not give details of planning permission for construction or change of use on nearby land, perhaps where adjoining land seems a likely candidate for development, or where perhaps a neighbour has applied to build a large extension overlooking your new garden. In these cases, further information outside the scope of a local authority search will be needed.

Water and drainage search

Your solicitor will apply to the local water authority for a search which will reveal:

- Whether the property is connected to mains water supply.
- Whether the property has a water meter.
- Whether the foul and surface water drain to a public sewer.
- The location of sewers and water mains in and around the property.
- Any risk of flooding due to overloaded public sewers, and risk of low water pressure.

This is a search to check drainage and fresh water supply arrangements. It does NOT cover aspects of potential high water level flooding. The Environment Agency have a very useful website that shows where flooding is common and/or extensive, or you could ask for a specific Flood Search if you have any concerns about this.

The water and drainage search will disclose whether any sewers or drains run within the boundaries of the property, which could affect any future building work you may wish to do. If, for example, you wish to extend the property over a drain, you would need to obtain approval to do this, or perhaps even re-direct the drain.

Environmental search

This search reveals matters of an environmental nature relating to the area in which the property stands. If there is nothing detrimental to report, the search will return with a 'Passed' certificate.

MONEY-SAVING TIP

If you are not taking out a mortgage or loan on a property, you are under no obligation to have searches carried out. If you know the area and have knowledge of the property, you may not need them. Discuss this with your solicitor before deciding.

Less common searches

In certain areas of the country, for example where mining has been prevalent, additional searches may be necessary. Your solicitor will advise you on which ones would be appropriate, but here are some of the less common searches:

• Index Map search
A check at the Land Registry to clarify the ownership of land. Your solicitor will know from the Land Registry entries who owns the property you are buying (assuming it is registered), but he may in addition wish to check who owns land around the property you are buying, for example a rear access route which is not part of the property but is used by the owners.
• Coal or Tin search
A check for the evidence or effects of underground mining in areas of the country where there has been a history of mining.
• Commons Registration search
A search to check whether any part of the property (or any access to it) is registered as Common Land.

• Highway search

In addition to the information in a local search regarding adopted highways, this search identifies the extent of the adjoining roads, paths or verges that are adopted and maintainable at public expense. If these areas are not adopted, then rights of way are required and there could be maintenance costs involved.

• Radon gas search

An enquiry is made to the National Radiological Protection Board to see if the property is known to be affected by radon gas.

• Chancel repair search

This search ascertains if the property could be liable to contribute to the cost of repairs to a church. Potentially, costs can be very high, but if there is a potential liability, then the sellers would be asked to provide indemnity insurance to protect against future claims.

Title information

Most properties built or transferred from one owner to another since 1925 will be registered at the Land Registry and will have been allocated a 'title number' for identification. If the property is not registered, your solicitor will let you know, and he will investigate the 'root of title' – the documents that show how the property has been legally passed to the current owner.

Your solicitor will apply to the Land Registry for a copy of the information registered against the property you are buying. This is referred to as a copy of the registered title, or registered entries. This document will confirm:

• The name of the owner and his address.
• Whether the property is freehold or leasehold. If it is leasehold it will give details of the lease, and a copy of the lease is usually held by the Land Registry.
• The price paid when the current owner purchased the property.

- Details of ownership, for example whether the owners are joint tenants or tenants in common.
- Details of any loan or mortgage (referred to as a Charge) secured against the property, including the date the loan was taken out and details of the lender.
- Any rights, restrictions or transfers registered against the property, and details of the documents that detail these. There may, for example, be a restrictive covenant registered against the title, stating that the owner should not build an extension. If the seller has done so, your solicitor may suggest taking out indemnity insurance to cover any future legal costs you might incur. A copy of any significant documents will be obtained by your solicitor.
- A basic plan of the property, showing the boundaries.

Additional enquiries

There may be aspects of the property or its sale that are not clear from the information supplied by the seller, and if this is the case, and it usually is, then your solicitor will raise additional enquiries. Below is an example of the sort of things that may need clarification:

- The seller has stated that both the right and left boundaries belong. This is presumably because the right-hand boundary abuts the communal parking area, but please confirm.
- Please confirm the seller has enjoyed uninterrupted use of the pathway to the rear of the property during his ownership, and that no contribution towards its maintenance and upkeep has ever been paid or demanded.
- Please confirm the seller's husband will sign the contract as occupier.
- Our local search has revealed planning permission for the rear and side extensions. Please provide completion certificates.

- You have supplied a FENSA certificate for the new windows to the front of the property. Are the rear windows the original windows?
- The agent's particulars state the bathroom fittings have been replaced. Did this replacement involve any new plumbing and/or electrical work?

Your solicitor should send you a copy of these enquiries, together with the replies when received.

STEP 2 – REPORTING TO YOU

Once your solicitor has gathered together all the relevant information about the property, he will report his findings to you. He will usually send a long letter or report, drawing your attention to any particular aspects of the property that you need to know about, for example any shared access routes or obligations on your part to maintain common areas with others.

You will be sent a copy of the Land Registry entries (as detailed above), together with a copy of the Land Registry plan, which will show the property in its entirety, but with little detail. The plot of land and the building itself will be outlined, together with any garage belonging, but it will not show how the building is divided into rooms. If you are buying a flat, the freehold land will be outlined, in other words the whole building or block, with the location of the part you are purchasing shown in a different colour and described in the Property Register section of the Land Registry entries.

You will also be sent the Fittings and Contents form, Property Information form, Energy Performance Certificate, copy searches and any other enquiry forms completed by the seller.

It is your obligation (and simple common sense) to read through all these documents carefully, and make a list of anything you are concerned about. If you do not understand any of the documents or the seller's replies to enquiries, ask for clarification.

MONEY-SAVING TIP

If you have any specific queries, let your solicitor know as soon as possible, so that he can save time by raising these along with his own enquiries.

Once your solicitor receives satisfactory replies to his enquiries, he will send you the Contract (or Agreement for Sale) for your signature and return.

If you are taking out a mortgage, your solicitor will receive a copy of your mortgage offer, which will set out details of the loan (including the term, interest rate and any restrictions or penalty clauses). He will usually outline to you the key points of the offer, then ask you to sign and return the official Mortgage Deed in readiness for completion. Your lender may also require you to formally accept the offer before taking out the mortgage; usually this means signing and returning an acceptance form.

Signing documents such as the contract or mortgage deed does not commit you to the purchase or the mortgage. Only when contracts are exchanged are they binding (see below) or, in the case of the mortgage, when the funds have been received. Your solicitor will hold the signed documents until they are needed.

STEP 3 – EXCHANGE OF CONTRACTS

The solicitors acting for both buyer and seller will now have duplicate contracts signed by their respective clients. Once a date for completion has been agreed (the date you will legally become the owner), the solicitors have a brief telephone conversation during which they insert the completion date on the contract and agree the deposit terms. The contracts are then dated and swapped (or exchanged), usually by post.

This is the exchange of contracts, and the point of no return. The contract is now legally binding – the seller must sell, and the buyer must buy. If you decide not to go ahead with the purchase you will be in breach of the contract, and you can be pursued for the purchase money, together with any interest and legal costs incurred. In lieu of the seller taking proceedings, it would be normal for the deposit to be forfeited.

Deposit and other money matters

At the point contracts are exchanged, the deposit is sent to the seller's solicitor, usually 10 per cent of the purchase price. You will need to ensure your solicitor has this money in his bank account by the day of exchange, so that he can send it on.

If you are selling a property simultaneously with your purchase, it is likely that the deposit received on your sale will be used as the deposit on your purchase, so you will not need to come up with funds for this, unless it is a higher amount.

Around the time of exchange, you should receive a Completion Statement from your solicitor, showing all the payments in and out, and the funds needed to be supplied by you to complete the purchase.

COMPLETION STATEMENT

Purchase of 123 The Street

Receipts		Payments	
Mortgage advance	50,000.00	Purchase price	200,000.00
Deposit	20,000.00	Search fees	350.00
Payment on account	250.00	Legal fees (inc VAT)	600.00
		Stamp Duty @ 1%	2,000.00
B/F from your sale	85,000.00	T/T fee	42.00
		Land Registry fees	280.00
Amount to complete	48,027.00	Land Registry searches	5.00
Total receipts	203,277.00	Total payments	203,277.00

In this example, £85,000 has been received from a related sale, which is going towards the purchase price.

The 'amount to complete' must be deposited with the solicitor before completion, in cleared funds. If you pay this by cheque, you will need to send this a week or so before completion, to allow time for your bank to clear the money into your solicitor's bank account.

Mortgage advance

Once contracts have been exchanged, your solicitor will send a Certificate of Title to your lender, confirming the date of completion and requesting funds to be released to his firm's bank account on the day of completion (or perhaps the day before). Lenders will usually need 5–10 days' notice before they will release the mortgage funds.

It is possible for exchange of contracts and completion to take place on the same day, but usually there is a week or so between, to allow for mortgage funds to be released.

Insurance

It is your responsibility to insure the property from the date contracts are exchanged – your lender will have stipulated this in the Mortgage Offer. Arrange your insurance in advance, and ring the insurance company or broker on the day of exchange to put the cover into effect.

STEP 4 – COMPLETION

This is the day you have been waiting for. Your solicitor will send the purchase funds by telegraphic transfer to the seller's solicitors. Once those funds are received, the seller's solicitor will confirm receipt (completion) and ring the selling agents (or current owners) to authorize them to release the keys to you.

Your solicitor will then ring you to tell you that completion has taken place, and the keys may be collected.

The Transfer document referred to earlier will now be sent to your solicitor. This is the document that transfers ownership of the property to you.

Stamp Duty

Your solicitor will now pay any Stamp Duty Land Tax (SDLT) payable on the purchase. The amount is a percentage of the purchase price (see page 54).

Remember, the percentage payable applies to the whole of the purchase price, not just the amount above the previous band rating. So, if the purchase price is £200,000, you will pay 1 per cent of £200,000, not 1 per cent on the balance over the £125,000 zero per cent threshold.

MONEY-SAVING TIP

If your purchase price is just over a SDLT threshold, you may be able to bring it into the lower band by separating part of the purchase price into chattels. For example, if your purchase price is £251,000 you will be in the 3 per cent Stamp Duty bracket. However, if you can exclude, say, the garden summer house (valued around £2,000) from the purchase price and pay for this separately, your purchase price will drop to £249,000 and be in the 1 per cent bracket, saving you a considerable sum of money. The value of the chattels has to be verifiable – it could be checked by the Inland Revenue – and of course the seller must agree to this arrangement.

Registration

After completion, your solicitor will check the Transfer document has been correctly signed, and then send it to the Land Registry with the appropriate fee. He will also send the mortgage deed and a certificate confirming payment of SDLT. The Land Registry will then amend the official register to show you as the new owner, and send your solicitor a copy of the new entries. A copy will be sent to you.

This is the only 'deed' that you need to prove ownership, although your solicitor may send you any historical documents he holds, for your interest.

DIY CONVEYANCING

We cannot end this section on conveyancing without mentioning that you can, if you are brave enough, handle the conveyance yourself.

Common practice implies that you need a solicitor for conveyancing in much the same way as you need a dentist to remove a tooth. However, there is no law that says you can't remove your own teeth, and similarly you are quite at liberty to handle the considerably less painful task of administering a property purchase (or sale, for that matter).

If you have common sense, want to save money, and have the time and necessary administrative skills, you may decide to do your own. But before you do, consider some of the pros and cons.

THE ADVANTAGES

The main advantage is the financial saving, which can be considerable. This will, however, be reduced if you are taking out a mortgage to fund your purchase, since your lenders will instruct their own solicitor if you are not employing one, and there are no prizes for guessing who will pay the fee.

If you have had a bad experience with a solicitor in the past, you may feel that you can do a better job. Solicitors do sometimes make mistakes and they are perhaps not as diligent as an interested party – you, for instance – might be. This diligence can be important, since such issues as proposed building works or new road schemes are only really unearthed by personal investigation.

Many people assume that the mysterious 'searches' will uncover anything important, and up to a point they do. But standard searches do not reveal everything, and there may be some aspects of your new home, or the area it is in, that are particularly important to you, and that require personal investigation.

THE DISADVANTAGES

If you do your own conveyance, you will almost certainly come up against opposition from lenders, and many will not process a loan application without details of your solicitor.

This is because lenders usually instruct the borrower's solicitor to act for them to ensure their interests are protected. The upshot of this is that you will be restricted to only those lenders who are happy to proceed with you directly.

In addition, the conveyancing system relies heavily on solicitors giving each other professional undertakings (promises) to do something crucial in the transaction, for example to repay an existing mortgage secured against the property you are buying. As an individual, your undertaking is not acceptable.

Perhaps the most important disadvantage is time, and the potential to make mistakes. This is why most people prefer to relax in the belief that the conveyance is being dealt with by someone who knows the system far better than they do, and is qualified to do the job. Personally, I am inclined to agree.

Do not underestimate the knowledge you will need to acquire to deal with a conveyance. If you get stuck part way through, and end up needing a solicitor to sort out the mess, this will be far more expensive than employing one in the first place.

IN CONCLUSION

If you are still keen to go it alone, a straightforward purchase of a registered, freehold property, preferably in a short chain, is best for the first timer. The purchase of a leasehold property is more complicated, not least because of the unfathomable jargon used in a lease, which may make it difficult for you to understand fully what you are agreeing to. But understand you must, to be sure the lease is sound and there are no unreasonable terms or charges.

There are several books on the market, and plenty of information on the Internet for DIY conveyancers, but do make sure the information you follow is up to date, and bear in mind that it would be difficult to cover in a book every conceivable scenario or problem that could arise outside the scope of a 'normal' conveyance. If you get stuck part way through, you will have nobody to go to for advice.

Finally, if you are not good at expressing yourself concisely, if you are daunted by officialdom, if you want to complete the purchase quickly, if you do not have plenty of spare time, if you are not prepared to read widely on the subject and if you are at all disorganized with your paperwork, don't even consider it.

IN SUMMARY

- Get the best quote for the conveyancing work by shopping around.
- Try to agree a fixed fee with your solicitor, especially for a leasehold purchase.
- Keep in touch with your solicitor regularly, and ask if there is anything you need to do to keep the matter moving ahead.
- Check that any documents you need to deal with are signed and returned promptly.
- Read everything.
- If you don't understand something, ask.
- Keep your solicitor informed of anything you arrange through the agents or with the seller.
- Be aware of the added costs involved, such as search fees and Stamp Duty, before you set your budget.

Chapter 9
JOINT PURCHASES

BUYING A PROPERTY WITH SOMEONE ELSE

Where two or more people buy a property together, they do so either as *joint tenants* or as *tenants in common*, which are the legal terms used to distinguish between those who co-own jointly and those who co-own separately. The term 'tenant' does not mean that you only have a tenancy or lease of the premises, and it applies to freehold purchases as well as leasehold.

JOINT TENANCY

This is the usual arrangement if you are buying as husband and wife, but can also be the case between unmarried couples and where more than two joint owners will own the property in equal shares, with none of them having a greater interest than the other.

If one of the owners dies, the other 'inherits' automatically. It is not possible for one party to leave his or her share of the property in a will to another person, or to sell his interest separately. It is irrelevant that one owner may make a greater contribution to the purchase or to paying any mortgage than the other.

Each buyer is treated as owning the whole of the property. No division of the property or the proceeds of a sale of the property is made, even if one party has contributed the whole or a greater proportion of the purchase price. On the death of one owner, his or her share transfers automatically to the other co-owner. Any gift or purported gift of a share in the property will not have any effect, unless there is a document signed by both buyers breaking the arrangement.

TENANTS IN COMMON

This arrangement is used when purchasers make unequal financial contributions to the purchase. Each buyer has his or her own share of the property, and the proportion each party holds is agreed at the time of purchase. For example, one of the buyers may contribute two thirds of the purchase price, and the other one third. Usually a Deed of Trust will be drawn up, showing the proportion of each purchaser. If the property is subsequently sold, each owner will receive their respective percentage of the net-sale proceeds.

Each owner can bequeath his interest in the property to another person, since ownership does not automatically pass to the surviving owner in the event of death. Instead, the share will form part of the deceased co-buyer's estate and will pass in accordance with his or her will, or in accordance with the rules applicable on a death if a will has not been made.

If the share passes to a third party (someone other than the other co-buyer) then that person can force a sale of the property to recover their inheritance.

WHICH IS RIGHT FOR YOU?

There are a number of matters to consider before deciding whether to opt for tenants in common or a joint tenancy. A joint tenancy is usual where the co-buyers are husband and wife, although this may not always be the case.

A tenancy in common with a Trust Deed may be preferable in the following circumstances:

- The co-buyers are not married.
- There is a child or children from a previous relationship.
- One buyer makes a greater contribution to the purchase price than the other.
- For tax planning reasons.

If you are buying as co-owners you should ensure your solicitor is fully aware of this, not least to ensure that you are both registered as proprietors (owners) of the property. A person not registered as an owner of the property may find that he or she has no rights to remain in the property if the relationship breaks down.

It is possible to avoid difficult situations as a result of any future separation by entering into an agreement drawn up between the co-owners.

COHABITATION AGREEMENT

This type of agreement is not in fact legally enforceable, but in essence it sets out the parties' intentions and clarifies their intended obligations towards one another. It may cover such matters as who owns what items of furniture and the agreement regarding contributions towards household bills and mortgage payments.

TRUST DEED

A Trust Deed is a legally enforceable document, and sets out most importantly the proportions which each co-owner has in the proceeds of a sale of the property. It may also contain agreements on monthly mortgage instalments and other outgoings, how improvements are to be financed and other matters. In addition, it may set out the agreement on how the parties agree to proceed if a co-owner wishes to sell up, so that the other(s) can buy.

Once the Trust Deed is signed, it is conclusive and the provisions cannot be changed without the agreement of all co-owners.

DO I NEED A WILL?

If you own property and you die, the lack of a will causes many problems. Your estate and possessions, including your share in any property, will not be divided as you would wish, but will normally pass to members of your family in various shares and proportions as the law from time to time decides.

Particularly if you are unmarried, your partner is not necessarily treated as being a spouse and may be excluded altogether from benefiting on your death.

A will is always a good idea, even if you don't own a property, but if you do, it is certainly something that should be done as soon as possible. Your solicitor will be able to recommend someone who can draw this up for you. There are DIY kits available online and even through stationers, but a solicitor will ensure that your wishes are clear and that the document is executed correctly, which is essential for it to be legally binding.

You may find that certain additions to your insurance will help to cover the drawing up of a will. Also, a free will service is offered to certain trade union members.

MONEY-SAVING TIP

During March and October, people over the age of 55 can have a will drawn up by a solicitor free of charge under the Free Wills Month scheme. The offer is applied to different towns and cities each year – see if your location is covered at freewillsmonth.org.uk.

IN SUMMARY

- Speak to your solicitor for advice on the type of ownership that will be best for you.
- Have a Trust Deed drawn up if appropriate.
- Make sure you both understand the implications of how the property is to be held.
- Make a will.

Chapter 10
MOVING

THE END IS IN SIGHT

Buying a home is exciting, but as the moving date looms ever closer it can seem that there are a hundred things to do and very little time to do them in.

Happily, much of the stress of moving can be reduced with advance planning, and if you are organized you can usually pre-empt any nasty surprises. Last-minute complications are the bane of every house move, but if you are well prepared and keep track of what is happening, you can usually get things back on track before a minor hiccup becomes a major disaster.

Moving a lifetime's collection of possessions from one place to another is physically demanding, and it can come as quite a shock to find just how exhausting it is, and how much you have accumulated over the years. If you hire a van for a DIY move, you can expect to handle every item you own several times – into a box or crate, onto the van, off the van, then out of the box or crate.

> **MONEY-SAVING TIP**
>
> If you have the energy or can rope in some help from friends or family, do your own removals. Not only will this be cheaper, but you are not tied down to a specific date – often organized far in advance of completion – by a removal company.

We'll deal with packing in more detail later in this chapter, but there are lots of other things you can do in advance of moving day, and on the day itself, to make it a smooth operation. For the well prepared, moving day is hard work, but satisfying – survived by good organization and a bit of luck. For those who make no preparation, chaos and confusion are inevitable.

Moving day should be a time to reap the benefits of all the effort put into finding and arranging the purchase of your new home, and with a bit of effort beforehand, it can be.

ADVANCE PREPARATIONS

Once you know the date you will be moving, you can start to let everyone know about your impending change of address. It's useful to get some change-of-address cards printed for this, and it's a good idea to leave a space to add reference numbers where necessary for service providers. Go through your home files and make a list of who you need to advise – here are some to get you started:

- Service suppliers (see below).
- Insurance companies.
- Bank / Building Society.
- Doctor, dentist and vet.
- TV Licensing Authority.
- Rental/HP companies.
- Tax Office.
- Employer.
- School.
- Family and friends.
- DVLC (you will need to produce your driving licence if you are hiring a van for the move, so take a copy before you send the original to be amended).

In most cases, all you need to do is to send a brief note or email showing your full name, the address you are moving from, the address you are moving to and any reference number to identify your account. Keep a copy of the letters and emails so that you know who has been advised, or make a list of who you have contacted, and keep that instead.

COUNTDOWN TO MOVING DAY

The following basic timetable should help you organize the major tasks and prepare yourself for the big move. It's far better to have a plan of action, rather than leaving everything to the last minute. Of course, if you are moving from rented accommodation you will need to give the required notice to your landlord, usually a month, but check your tenancy agreement.

TWO WEEKS BEFORE MOVING DAY

- Clear out the garage, shed and loft of anything that needs to be disposed of, and pack everything else.

- Sort through cupboards and wardrobes (especially children's) to see if any items need to be given away, sold or thrown out.
- Take cuttings of favourite garden plants, or divide them (you should not remove the whole plant).
- Start winding down the amount of food in the freezer.

ONE WEEK BEFORE MOVING DAY

- Return DVD rentals/library books (if moving to a different area).
- Dismantle structures as necessary, such as greenhouse or wardrobes.
- Order pet tags with new address.
- Arrange for disconnection of appliances, such as gas fire or cooker, to take place before moving day.

TWO DAYS BEFORE MOVING DAY

- Defrost fridge and freezer.

THE DAY BEFORE MOVING DAY

- Take down pictures, curtains and poles (if not included in the sale).
- Remove any fittings not included in the sale, such as light fittings or shades.
- Roll up rugs.
- Make sure you have enough petrol in your car, and some cash.

The less you have to do on the day of the move, the better. If that means eating out the evening before, or picnicking on a take-away in the only room left with somewhere to sit, then this is far better than having to clear the kitchen or take down fittings the next day when you will have quite enough to do as it is.

TRANSFERRING SERVICES

If you are taking on services for the first time, some suppliers may insist that you pay a connection charge or security deposit before they will accept you as a customer. Also, you may need to give more than the minimum required notice to allow time for your application to be processed.

> **MONEY SAVING TIP**
> With so many service providers out there, moving home is a good time to take a look at the competition and see if you can get a better deal with a different supplier.

TELEPHONE

Your telephone supplier can usually give you a new number in advance of the move, and then transfer the service from the old number to the new one on the day. You should give at least two weeks' notice. If your new property does not already have a telephone line, arranging connection is simply a matter of contacting your telephone provider and giving them at least seven days notice of a convenient connection date. There will be an installation charge for provision of the new line.

BROADBAND

It's usually easier (and cheaper) to stay with the same service provider when you move, particularly if you are still under contract. Let them know as soon as possible that you will be moving, since some require at least one month's notice. If your provider insists that you restart your contract when you move, look around to make sure you have the best deal.

COUNCIL TAX

Contact the council to whom you presently pay Council Tax. Advise them of your current address and the date you will be vacating it, and the address you are moving to. The council will calculate the relevant daily charge for the time you remain in your existing property, and open a new account for your new property if it is within their governing area. If you are moving to a different part of the country, you will need to contact the local authority there.

> **MONEY-SAVING TIP**
> Is the Council Tax band correct? If the band on the house you are buying is higher than comparable properties, you may be able to get it changed. If you have been paying too much tax on your old property, you could claim back a lump sum of overpayment. Use the Valuation Office Agency website for England and Wales, or the Scottish Assessors Association for Scotland to check.

ELECTRICITY

You need to give the electric company that supplies the power at your existing property at least two working days' notice of your intended move. This is the minimum notice you are required to give by law, but ideally you should give at least a week. Contact them and give your account number and current address. They may then visit the property on the day you vacate to take a final meter reading; in practice, they rarely do this, and it is up to you to take a final reading before you leave.

Send the final reading to your supplier, advising them of your new address and asking them to send a final bill. If you pay by Direct Debit, they should debit your account with the final balance and close the account.

Take a meter reading at the new property when you move in, and give this to the supplier there, so that they can set up a new account for you. Keep a note of the meter reading, in case there is any dispute about who owes what.

GAS

The system for changing your address with your gas supplier is much the same as for electricity (see above). If any gas appliances, such as a cooker, need to be disconnected before you move, arrange an appointment for this in advance with a Gas Safe registered engineer.

If you use gas cylinders rather than mains gas, any appliances not included in the sale need to be carefully disconnected, and the cylinders turned off. You will probably have arranged to leave the cylinders for the new owner, but if not, return them to the supplier to reclaim any deposit paid.

WATER

Water and drainage costs are either calculated on a daily rate, or by meter readings.

Contact the company that currently supplies your water and drainage. Tell them your current address, the address you are moving to and the date of the move. If you have a water meter, give them the meter reading. The company then prepares a final bill for your current address by either using the meter reading or calculating the number of days the service has been used.

If you are moving within the same supply area, the company will also open an account for your new address. You will need to let them know the meter reading at your new address on completion day, if the supply is metered.

If you are moving to a different supply area, contact the relevant company there and advise the date you will be moving in, and the meter reading if the supply is metered.

MONEY-SAVING TIP

If your water consumption is low (for example if you live alone), consider having a water meter installed at your new home if there is not one there already. You have a right to have a meter installed free of charge, unless this would be impractical or unreasonably expensive. Your bills will usually be lower if they are an accurate depiction of your usage, rather than based on average family daily rates.

POST

Your local post office can arrange for your mail to be redirected to your new home. You may think you have advised everybody of your new address, but being sure all your mail is automatically redirected gives peace of mind in case someone has been overlooked. You can apply for redirection by completing the appropriate form, available in post offices, or apply online. The charge for this service depends on the length of time redirection is arranged, and it is applied to each surname, so Mr and Mrs Green would be charged one fee for both people, whereas Mr Green and Miss Smith would be charged a fee for each surname.

Whenever a piece of redirected mail arrives, contact the sender to advise them of your new address.

INSURANCE

Your contents insurance policy may cover your possessions whilst they are in transit between your old home and new home, but do check. If not, most removal companies can arrange this for you, for a fee, although this may not be on a 'new for old' replacement basis. Be sure to read the small print with either cover, since it is common practice to exclude 'owner-packed' goods, which could leave many of your most precious possessions uninsured.

Be aware also that insurance policies which cover goods during removal often stipulate a time limit for making a claim, so even if you don't unpack everything straight away, check to make sure nothing is damaged when you arrive at your new home.

If you hire a van to do the move yourself, you will need insurance to cover loss or damage to the vehicle. This will probably be arranged through the hire firm, but it can carry a large excess figure (the part of any repair costs you would have to pay), so shop around if you can.

If you borrow a van privately, from a friend or relative, make sure you are adequately insured to drive it AND your driving licence permits you to drive such a vehicle. Unless you hold an HGV licence, you cannot hire or drive a vehicle of more than 7.5 tonnes of laden weight.

PACKING

If you are doing all the packing yourself, and not employing a removal company to do it for you, it is advisable to start the job at least two weeks before the moving date. Almost everyone underestimates the time it will take, so you can be fairly sure it will take longer than you anticipate.

First things first, you will need boxes to put all your possessions into. You can buy or hire these from removal companies, or online, or you can ask your local supermarket or other shops if they have any spare they want to get rid of, although this is less likely nowadays. To estimate how many boxes you will need, do a rough reckoning on how many you will need for each room, then double it!

Rather than packing up each room in turn, it is better to pack non-essentials first, especially those things you will not be in a hurry to unpack at the other end. That way you can pack away a lot of things that are not used on a daily basis well in advance of the moving date, and leave these boxes unpacked at the other end until you decide at leisure where to put the contents.

It is vital to label the boxes as you pack, so that you know what is in them. You may initially remember what each box holds, but as more and more are filled and sealed it can start to get confusing. If you need to retrieve something that has already been packed, you can bet it will be in the last box you look in.

Label boxes 'bedroom 1', 'study' and so on as you fill them, to ensure they will be unloaded straight into the right room at your new home, and you can avoid wasting time and energy moving them again. For this system to work, the removal men need to know what each room in your new home will be used for, since it may not be immediately obvious to them. The easiest way to do this is to stick a note on the door of each room, identifying the room as 'study' or 'bedroom 1'.

Moving home is a good opportunity to have a bit of a clear out, so take old clothes, books and toys to the local charity shop. Sort through kitchen cupboards and medicine cabinets to get rid of any goods that are out of date, and clear the garage and loft

It's obviously better to do this when packing, rather than moving everything and then sorting it at the other end.

> **MONEY-SAVING TIP**
>
> If you have a sort-out in plenty of time before the move, you may be able to sell a lot of your unwanted items online, through the local media or at car boot sales.

Take care to label boxes containing fragile items, so that they are not loaded under heavy boxes, and the 'right way up' should be clearly displayed if it is important. Some sort of padding will be needed, so ask neighbours and friends to save their newspapers, and you could also utilize spare bedding, pillows, cushions or blankets to protect against damage.

It's a good idea to have one 'do not remove' box, with things you do not want to go in the removal van, including, for example:

- Kettle, mugs and tea and coffee.
- Light bulbs.
- Toilet roll, soap and a towel.
- Cleaning materials.
- Snacks, biscuits, bottled water.
- Children's toys.
- Telephone number of solicitor, selling agents, removal company.

If you arrive at your new home before the removal van, which is quite likely, it might also be useful to transport the vacuum cleaner separately, so that the carpets can be given a quick once over before they are covered up with furniture and boxes.

If a removal firm is packing for you, they will probably come the day before the move to pack, then return on the day to load up.

When the removal van arrives, it makes sense to synchronize the loading so that those things that are needed first at the other end, such as rugs and wardrobes, go onto the van last. The removal men will probably not think to do this for you, so you need to be in charge of the loading order.

REMOVALS

Doing it yourself is the cheapest option, or you could hire a 'man and a van' which gives you an extra pair of hands to help with moving heavy furniture and white goods. This is a much cheaper option, but there are a few disadvantages:

- Loading and unloading will take longer, since you are unlikely to be as experienced as the removals staff.
- You will probably need to make more than one journey, because the van will be too small to take everything in one go, and you will not have the experience to fully use the van space efficiently.
- You are more likely to damage something, because you will not be used to loading and handling.

- It is physically strenuous – washing machines and wardrobes are even heavier than they look.
- It is emotionally more exhausting because you have more to think about.
- Negotiating stairs and awkward exits with heavy goods may need lifting gear you will not have.
- Any last-minute jobs (and you can be sure there will be some) will cause delays if you are preoccupied with loading and unloading.

Hiring a professional removal firm is your other option, although this can be expensive. Whether or not to choose this option will depend on the distance involved, how fit you are, how much furniture you have to move and whether much of it is heavy or awkward to lift.

If you do decide to use a removal firm, get several quotes from different companies. The standard of service varies between companies, and so does the price. Large companies offer a more comprehensive service than just transporting packed boxes from one place to another.

MONEY-SAVING TIP

If you are moving to a different area, don't just get quotes from local firms. Say you are moving from London to Cornwall: the Cornish firm is likely to be far cheaper than the London based firm. Both will charge for a two-way trip, whichever way round it is.

Most professional removal firms are members of the British Association of Removers, and you should ask them to confirm this to you. This membership means that you are protected by the Association's Code of Practice.

An assessor from your chosen removal company will usually visit your property to gauge the amount of furniture and effects to be removed, or sometimes you can complete a form online. Be sure to mention everything to be moved, including the contents of the loft or garage, or you may find that the van they send is too small. If you are moving to somewhere that has limited access – perhaps the road is narrow so parking a large van could be a problem – do mention this so that the removal company can be prepared.

The amount of notice needed to book a removal firm varies; some only need a week, whereas others ask for a month. Friday is the most popular day for moving, since this is the day when property completions most usually take place, and the end of the month is always busy. Moving at the weekend can cause problems if you need a plumber or electrician to connect services, and bear in mind that your solicitor's office will be closed.

Removal men usually arrive early, so set your alarm. Loading the contents of an average three-bedroom house takes in excess of three hours (allowing for tea breaks), so the aim is to clear the property by noon, in time for the arrival of the new occupiers and their removal van. By the time you arrive at your new home, the previous owners should be on the way to their new home, and so on.

Before you leave your old home for the last time, take a good look around to make sure you haven't forgotten anything. It's surprisingly easy to miss a picture or rug. Turn off the heating (unless you have arranged otherwise with the new owners), and make sure windows are closed and entrance doors locked. Take meter readings, then drop the keys off with the selling agent – or whatever arrangement you have made.

MOVING IN

Having survived the process of moving out of your old home, which is 80 per cent of the work, you can now move smoothly into your new one.

The removal van will probably take longer than you to arrive, giving you time to have a cup of tea and something to eat before starting the unloading and packing. When you get to your new home, take a good look round the property to make sure everything is as it should be, and if anything is wrong speak to your solicitor. Take meter readings and check that the heating and other appliances are working, and that the telephone has been connected. Ring your own mobile phone to check the number is correct.

When the removal van arrives, don't automatically start unpacking the first box that comes off it, even though hopefully you will have loaded the van in some order. Instead, have a plan of what to deal with in order of importance, so that you are not worn out by unpacking incidentals before you get round to unpacking the things you need immediately.

Food and sleep are a priority at the end of a tiring move, so make up the beds and unpack essential kitchen equipment first. The rest can be dealt with afterwards.

Welcome to your new home.

IN SUMMARY

- Be organized – if you've never written a list before, now is the time to start.
- Get several quotes from removal companies, or van-hire firms.
- Check your insurance.
- Do everything you can in advance. Don't leave anything to the last minute.
- Packing will take at least twice as long as you imagine, so give yourself plenty of time.
- Keep notes of meter readings.

INDEX